Lars Edlund - MODUS VETUS

Sight Singing and Ear-Training in Major/Minor Tonality

Translation revised by Alan Stout, Professor at Northwestern University, Evanston, Illinois

**AB NORDISKA MUSIKFÖRLAGET
EDITION WILHELM HANSEN STOCKHOLM**

Wilhelm Hansen, Musik-Forlag
København

Norsk Musikforlag A/S
Oslo

J. & W. Chester Ltd.
London

Edition Wilhelm Hansen
Frankfurt a. M.

Edition Wilhelm Hansen/Chester Music New York Inc.
Distribution: Magnamusic-Baton Inc.

NMS 6399

PREFACE

This textbook offers exercises in ear-training. Although primarily intended to be used in schools which specialize in music, it also can be used in elementary schools, high schools, and junior colleges. Applicants for admission to colleges and conservatories will find the easier exercises helpful when preparing for entrance examinations in ear-training. (This applies chiefly to the sections on Melody Reading and Rhythmic Exercises). Many of the exercises also can be used for private study, even though this book is not always decisive in their use or adaptation. The teachers and teaching assistants should complement and vary any material which is necessary for comprehensive use.

The chief goal of ear-training is to develop complete familiarity with the melodic, rhythmic, and harmonic sense of musical tones. A book on this subject should contain material on all these separate aspects, but the *studies of each aspect should be cultivated simultaneously throughout the course.* The intimate connection of this entire subject with practical music-making should be obvious, however, its importance cannot be stressed sufficiently. If ear-training is taught in a comprehensive way, it will be a highly integrated type of training which will include elements from several other branches of musical theory-melody writing, harmony, counterpoint, and the elements of musical form. These are combined into one category for this subject: Ear-training.

The book is divided into four sections:
I. Melody Reading Exercises
II. Rhythm Exercises
III. Figured Bass Exercises
IV. Keyboard Harmony Exercises

Once again it must be stressed that, as far as possible, all these aspects should be studied simultaneously. (The introduction to the Melody Reading Exercises gives further reason why this is true.) The index on page 6 gives some general suggestions how this can be accomplished.

The purpose of each section of the book is explained at its outset and instructions are given for practical methods to be followed. All work must be approached in a practical manner in order for this book to be regarded as an exercise in musical craftsmanship. MODUS VETUS - "the old way". Since the textbook on free-tonal melody reading was entitled *Modus Novus* (1963), *Modus Vetus* seemed an appropriate title for a textbook on practical music-making in major/minor tonality. One might say that this is a book published two centuries too late! Major/minor tonality has lost most of its basic meaning as a structural principle in contemporary music. Yet it is still necessary for us to study this subject methodically. As long as Bach, Mozart, and Beethoven are played and mean so much to us, we are obliged to study their "vocabulary".

In designing certain parts of the Melody Reading section, the author has been stimulated greatly by the works of the Danish composer, Jørgen Jersild, on the teaching of solfege (1), a debt which I gratefully acknowledge.

I also wish to express my sincere thanks to Eva Eklund, my colleague at the Royal Academy of Music in Stockholm, who has examined my manuscript critically.

Lars Edlund

(1) Ear Training - Basic Instruction in Melody and Rhythm reading (Wilhelm Hansen - G. Schirmer, New York)

CONTENTS

Correlation of various sections for simultaneous study ... 6

MELODY READING EXERCISES:

Introduction ... 7
Chapter I From the tonic to the major third ... 8
II From the major third to the tonic ... 10
III From the tonic to the minor third ... 13
IV From the minor third to the tonic ... 15
V Major and minor in the same example ... 18
VI Major third with neighboring tones ... 20
VII Minor third with neighboring tones ... 26
VIII Summary on intervals ... 30
IX A. Major and minor thirds ... 33
B. Diminished triads ... 35
X Five-tone scale in major with neighboring tones ... 37
XI Five-tone scale in minor with neighboring tones ... 47
XII Arpeggiated cadences ... 60
XIII The major scale ... 62
XIV The minor scale ... 80
XV Melodies not in major/minor tonality ... 93
XVI The dominant seventh chord ... 104
XVII The dominant ninth chord ... 121
    The dominant ninth chord with a lowered ninth and the root omitted (a diminished seventh chord). Secondary seventh chords. Diminished third in conjunction with the Neapolitan sixth chord.

RHYTHM EXERCISES ... 166

FIGURED BASS EXERCISES ... 180

KEYBOARD HARMONY EXERCISES ... 193

HARMONIC EXERCISES IN CONNECTION WITH THE MELODIES SUGGESTED METHOD ... 203

Source of melodies in Melody Reading Exercises ... 205

Key to Figured Bass Exercises ... 208

Suggestions for general correlation of Melody Reading, Rhythm, and Keyboard Harmony Exercises.[1]

Melody Reading Exercises	Rhythm Exercises	Keyboard Harmony Exercises (or aural tests in chords and dictation)
Chap. I – II	Series I – II	Example 1 – 2
„ III – V	„ III – IV	„ 1 – 2
„ VI	„ V – VI	„ 3 – 15
„ VII – XII	„ VII	„ 3 – 15
„ XIII	„ VII	„ 16 – 21
„ XIV – XV	„ VIII	„ 16 – 21
„ XVI	„ VIII	„ 16 – 21
„ XVII	„ IX – X	„ 22 – 45

[1] Work with the Figured Bass Exercises should be done gradually at a pace suited to the student.

MELODY READING EXERCISES

This section comprises the largest part of the book. The material has been designed primarily to develop a feeling for tonality. If tonal relations in melodies are to be understood properly, more is required than a mere facility in singing isolated melodic intervals. The student therefore should study the Keyboard Harmony Exercises, page 193, and the Figured Bass Exercises, page 180, at the same time as the Melody Reading Exercises. For those students who cannot play the piano at all, these exercises may be used as exercises in ear-training (see the introduction to each section). The Rhythm Exercises, page 166, should also be studied simultaneously.

The table on page 6 gives suggestions for ways in which the various sections may be studied simultaneously. These correlations can and should be applied somewhat differently by different students. The Melody Reading examples can be used for dictation, although they are intended primarily for singing. In the later chapters of this section some melodies are hard to sing, not only because of their difficult intervals and complicated rhythms but also because of their wide ranges or because they are inherently instrumental. Even so they still should be sung whenever possible. If the range is too great octaves may be transposed. These melodies at least can be used for dictation. Although most of the melodies are vocal in character, the author has not restricted himself only to such melodies.

The melodies also can supply material for harmonic exercises, consisting of basis aural harmonic analysis with practice in keyboard harmony. On page 203 are suggestions for further use.

The sources of these melodies are given on page 205. Melodies not listed there have been composed by the author.

I. From the tonic to the major third

Any given note can be treated as the tonic

Tonal material etc.

Begin on each degree of the chromatic scale and sing upwards to the major third, naming the notes.
Choose several melodies in this chapter for harmonic practice like the method on page 203.

Melodies

Copyright © 1967 by Nordiska Musikförlaget, Stockholm
English version
Copyright © 1974 by Nordiska Musikförlaget, Stockholm, Sweden

II. From the major third to the tonic

Any given note can be treated as a major third

Tonal material  etc.

Begin on each degree of the chromatic scale and sing downwards to the major third, naming the notes.
Choose several melodies in this chapter for harmonic practice like the method on page 203.

Melodies:

The following examples begin on the second degree of the major scale. The aim here is to treat any given note as the second degree of the scale. Practice each example in two ways:

(1) Determine the key and play its tonic. Then sing the example. Work through examples 16-24 in this way.

(2) Play the first note and determine the tonic yourself - in this case a major second downwards. Then sing the example.

III, From the tonic to the minor third

Tonal material  etc.

Begin on each degree of the chromatic scale and sing upwards to the minor third, naming the notes.

Choose several melodies in this chapter for harmonic practice like the method on page 203.

Melodies:

IV. From the minor third to the tonic

Any given note can be treated as a minor third.

Begin on each degree of the chromatic scale and sing downwards to the minor third, naming the notes.

Melodies:

The following examples begin on the second degree of the minor scale.
Practice each example according to the instructions on page 12.

Choose several melodies in this chapter for harmonic practice like the method on page 203.

V. Major and minor in the same example

Tonal material That which was used previously.

Choose several melodies in this chapter for harmonic practice like the method on page 203.

1a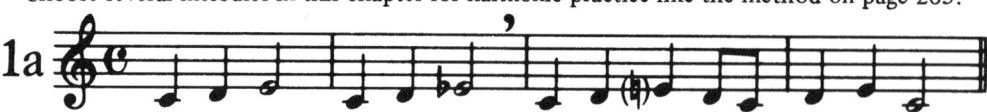

1b

2a

2b

3a

3b

VI. Major third with neighboring tones
Rising and falling leadingtone
Don't forget to choose several melodies for harmonic practice like the method on page 203.

The major third, the interval from the first to the third degrees of the major scale, has half steps on either side of its notes. One leads upwards from below to the tonic of the scale, and one leads downwards from above from the fourth to the third. In this context both these half steps have a strong leading tendency - to the tonic and to the third respectively. The note below the tonic is usually called the leading tone of the scale. So we are working now with the following group of notes:

The F (subdominant) and the B (leading tone) in this example each form a melodic digression from a starting point - E and C respectively, to which they return. The tendency of these "changing" notes would be more obvious if the above notes in the group were harmonized. *Sing and play the following harmonizations in various major keys, paying close attention to the leading tones in both voice and piano.*

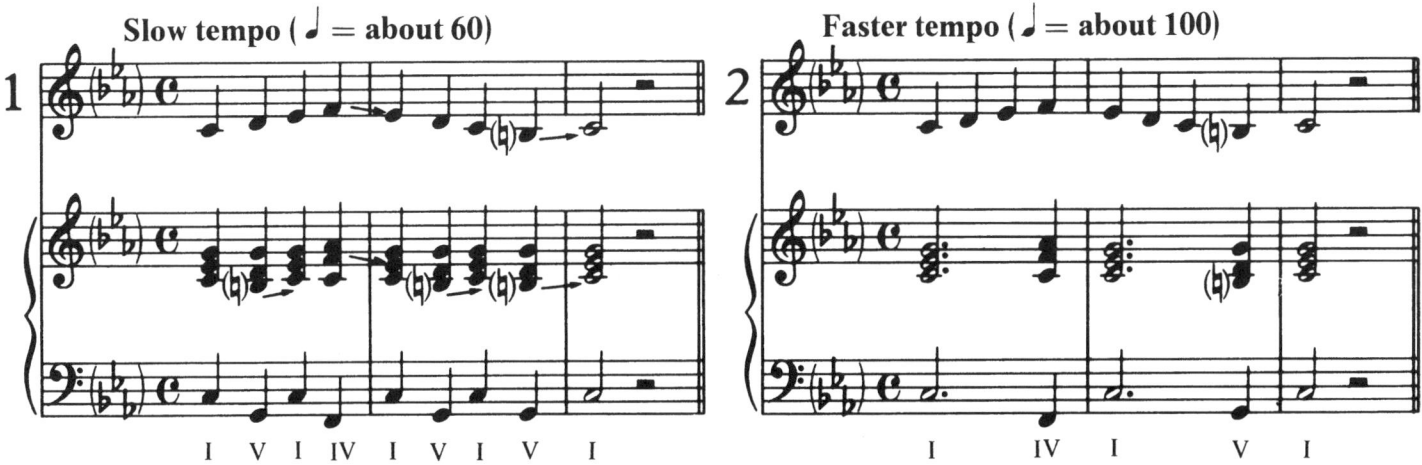

Note: In the faster example certain notes have not been harmonized. They act as so-called passing tones between two chord tones, thus giving a more flowing movement to the rhythm.

In Example 3 the dominant seventh (V^7) is included. This means that both the subdominant, which falls, and the leading tone, which rises, are found in the chord, still further emphasizing the tendency of the chord to move towards the tonic. Regarding the I^6_4 in Ex. 4, refer to Keyboard Harmony Exercise No. 10.

Exercise:

Play V^7-I (in different keys) and sing the subdominant and the leading tones. Try to find the B and the F in the V^7 chord without repeating these notes once the entire chord has been played.

Melodies:

(1) Regarding all melodies which do not begin on the tonic, see the instructions in Chapter II, page 12.

Use as much of the previous chordal material as possible with the subdominant triad (IV) and its inversions (IV^6 and IV$^6_4$) with the cadential I$^6_4$ chord (I$^6_4$-V) and also the dominant seventh chord (V^7 with its inversions (V$^6_5$, V$^4_3$ and V$^4_2$).

VII. Minor third with neighboring tones

Tonal material:

The interval F-E♭ in the above example does not have the same downward-leading tendency as it has in a major key. Yet the F does have a strong downward tendency when given the function of a dominant seventh.

Exercise:

(1) Sing and name these notes in various minor keys.
(2) Play, also starting on many different tones, the harmonizations in Chapter VI, page 21, in minor, observing the accidentals in parentheses. Sing the appropriate melodies!

Melodies:

Use the chordal material in Keyboard Harmony Exercises Nos. 1-15 (possibly also Nos. 16-25) in as many ways as possible.

VIII. Summary on intervals

On the basis of the tonal material used so far, we can classify the intervals encountered as follows:

SECOND

Major second (a diatonic [1]) whole step):

Minor second (a diatonic half step):

THIRD

Major third (2 diatonic whole steps):

Minor third (1 + 1/2 or 1/2 + 1 diatonic steps):

(1) A diatonic step is the distance between two neighboring tones with different letter names with or without accidentals.

FOURTH

Perfect fourth (1 + 1 + 1/2 or 1/2 + 1 + 1 or 1 + 1/2 + 1 diatonic steps):

Diminished fourth (1/2 + 1 + 1/2 diatonic steps):

Exercise:
The following exercise can be used to memorize the intervals. Write a chromatic scale:

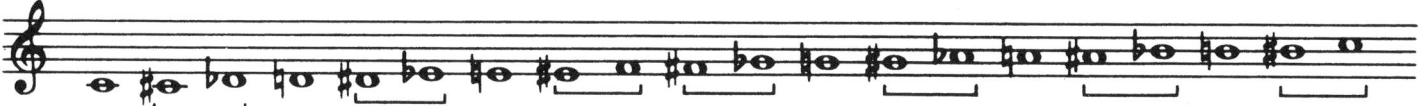

Write the above intervals upwards and downwards from each note in this chromatic scale.

A good knowledge of intervals implies quick recognition of any interval in the printed music and an ability to sing it at sight. This exercise is often applied only to isolated intervals. But it is by no means certain that skill in singing isolated intervals guarantees good sight reading of complete melodies. There are several reasons for this:

1) A melody is much more than a mechanical succession of larger and smaller intervals. When we read a literary text, we grasp syllables and whole words at a single glance, we see them as units, shapes. The same technique should be applied to reading music. Here the shapes are made up of melodic motives and phrases. But vital to the reading of major/minor melodies is the ability to see and feel the tonal quality of such shapes and to spot those notes which are "magnetic", thereby giving the other notes direction and function.

2) In major/minor tonality each interval always has some kind of tonal quality. The same interval can have several different tonal meanings, the response evoked being entirely different in different contexts.

3) In isolated intervallic exercises we ignore rhythm, which plays a great but subtle part in a melody. Rhythm also strongly influences our response to an interval. One reason for this is that rhythm often is related closely to the harmonic development of a melody.

4) A good command of isolated intervals (the ability to "hear" them mentally and to sing them from the printed page) is therefore only one requirement for good sight reading. This command is important, but it is not enough in itself. *In actual practice there is constant interplay between this knowledge and a perception of the tonal and rhythmic shapes and sequences.*

Note:

THE INTERVAL EXERCISE USING THE NOTES OF THE CHROMATIC SCALE, WHICH WAS RECOMMENDED ON THE PREVIOUS PAGE, SHOULD BE REPEATED WITH EACH NEW INTERVAL YOU ENCOUNTER IN THE MUSIC BELOW.

The preceeding chapters and exercises have stressed the importance of being able to determine the key in each example and thus identify the function of any given note in that key: Whether it is the tonic, the leading tone, the major third, the second, etc. These terms, in the mental picture we form of a note, always must have definite meaning, depending on the position of the note in relation to the tonic and other important notes. Any given note implies either potential movement or rest.

For example, take the note D. It may be the:

(1) Keynote or tonic (first degree of the scale):

(2) Leading tone (seventh degree of the scale):

(3) Major third:

(4) Minor third:

(5) Dominant seventh of the key, which is also the subdominant (fourth degree of the scale):

IX. A. Major and minor triads
B. Diminished triads

A.

Since the triad is emphasized greatly in the following chapters, it is presented here in a special section which should be prepared carefully. The triads in Nos. 1 - 9 are shown in root position (the root of the chord is the lowest note in the chord). Nos. 10 - 18 are in first inversion (the third of the chord is the lowest note) and Nos. 19 - 27 are in second inversion (the fifth of the chord is the lowest note). The term location refers to the highest note of the chord. Thus Nos. 1 - 9 have fifth location, 10 - 19 have octave location, and 19 - 27 have third location. No. 28 is in root position and third location, etc.

Exercise:

Describe position and location for triads in Nos. 29 - 40.

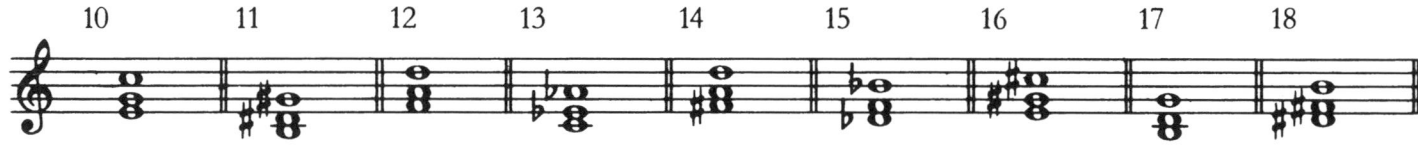

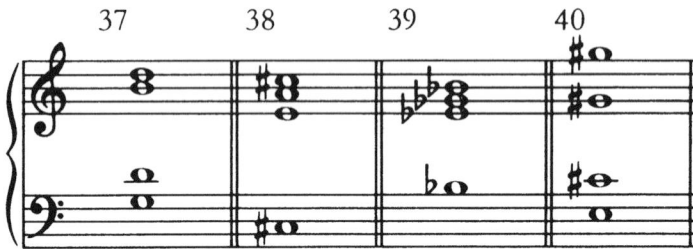

The tonic of the triad is easy to determine if the chord is in root position: That is, when the bass note and the tonic are identical. Determining the tonic in the inversions will take perhaps a little longer. A visual aid: The tonic is the top note in the interval of a fourth.

Exercise:

The triads on page 33 should be practiced as outlined in Nos. 1 - 5 below:

1) Play the triads on the piano. Sing the notes of each triad by name while the tones are still sounding on the piano. Check by playing the tonic alone.

2) Practice singing the third of each triad in the same way.

3) Do the same with the fifth of each triad.

4) Write the notation of triads 1 - 40 on a separate sheet of paper: (1) C major, (2) E minor, (3) C minor, etc. Close the textbook. Play only the tonic in each triad and then sing the complete triad by naming the notes.

5) The following numbers show the intervals used in the triad on the next page, determined from the tonic. The arrows indicate direction of movement.

  a) 1↗3↗5 c) 5↘3↘1 e) 3↘1↗5
  b) 1↗5↘3 d) 5↘1↗3 f) 3↗5↘1

Play triads 1 - 40 in turn. Sing each triad, naming the notes, according to (a) above. Check afterwards by playing (a). Then do the same with (b) through (f).

In addition, the following exercises are recommended:

6) Play any note on the piano. Sing major and minor triads according to (a) - (f) in (5) above by naming the notes, beginning each of the triads on the note you have played. This is a rather difficult exercise but a very effective one. The result of this exercise starting from the note F is shown on page 35.

7) Notate broken major and minor triads as shown in (a) - (f) above, but change the tonic for each triad. Sing the name of the notes after you have played only the first note of each triad. Check your work on the piano!

B.

B. The diminished triad consists of two minor thirds, the interval between the upper and lower notes forming a diminished fifth. According to major/minor tonal conventions, a diminished interval is a dissonance which must be resolved to consonance. If we look at the diminished triad formed on the seventh degree of the major scale (the leading tone), we find that the interval between the outside notes, the dimished fifth, is formed from the two "tendency tones" we have discussed previously. The customary resolution of this chord is therefore:

Notice that this diminished triad consists of the three upper intervals found in an ordinary dominant seventh:

Therefore in its harmonic function the diminished triad is a dominant seventh with the tonic left out, or a so-called imperfect dominant. The omitted tonic is symbolized by the zero following the function symbol in the figured bass. The imperfect dominant is perhaps most commonly used in second inversion - that is, with the fifth of the V^7 chord as its bass note:

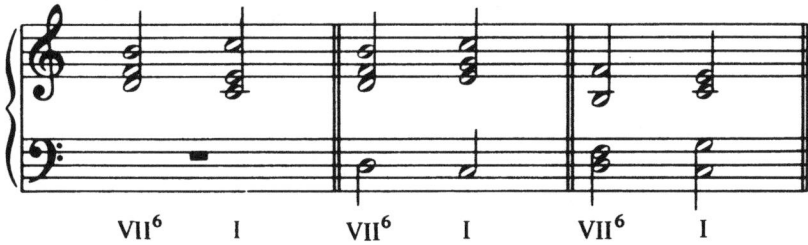

See Keyboard Harmony Exercises, No. 14, for additional work.

Exercise:

The diminished triads below can be practiced in the following way:
1) Determine the omitted V⁷ root for each triad, together with the key to which it customarily resolves.
2) Sing the triads and their common resolutions to tonic major, naming the notes, as in the following example:

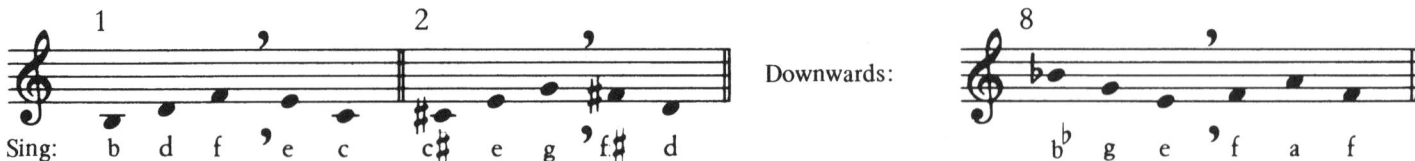

(If you like, you can play the roots of the dominant seventh and the tonic chords with the left hand on the piano. Then the harmonic context will become much clearer.)

(3) Sing the triads in the same way as in (2), but with resolution to tonic minor.

X. Five-tone scale in major with neighboring tones

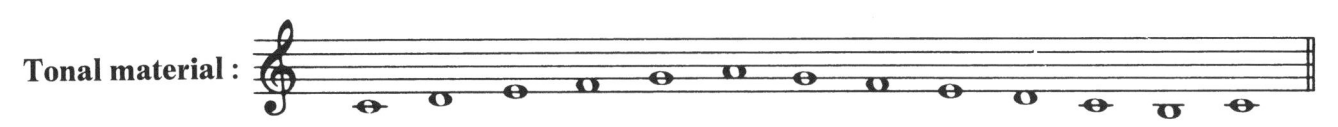

Tonal material:

Play the following harmonizations of these notes. Sing the melodies and practice them in several keys.

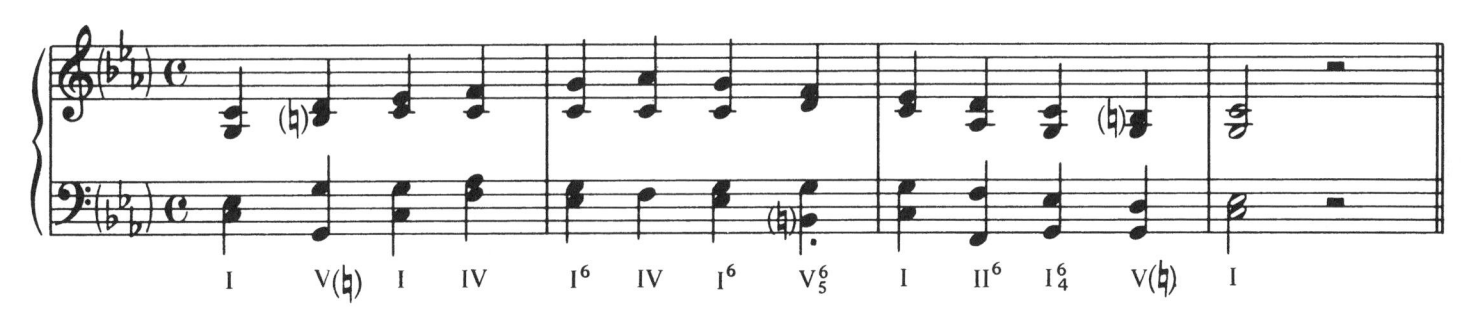

I   V(♮)   I   IV   I⁶   IV   I⁶   V⁶₅   I   II⁶   I⁶₄   V(♮)   I

2)   2)   1)   2)   3)

I   I⁶   IV   I⁶₄   V⁷(♮)   I

¹) Neighboring tone - also called auxiliary tone when it goes back to the original note.

²) Passing tone - moves by step and passes between two harmonic tones.

³) The C here can be called an accented passing tone or an appoggiatura to the harmony note B.

The unifying factor in this group of notes is the major triad, or the first, third, and fifth degrees of the scale:

(1) Passing tone
(2) Neighboring tone

Melodies:

8. Da pacem, Domine, da pacem, Domine, in diebus nostris.

Da pacem, Domine, da pacem, Domine, in diebus nostris.

40

Drei Sonnen sah ich am Himmel steh'n, hab lang und fest sie angesehn.

Allegro scherzoso (♩ = 112)

23

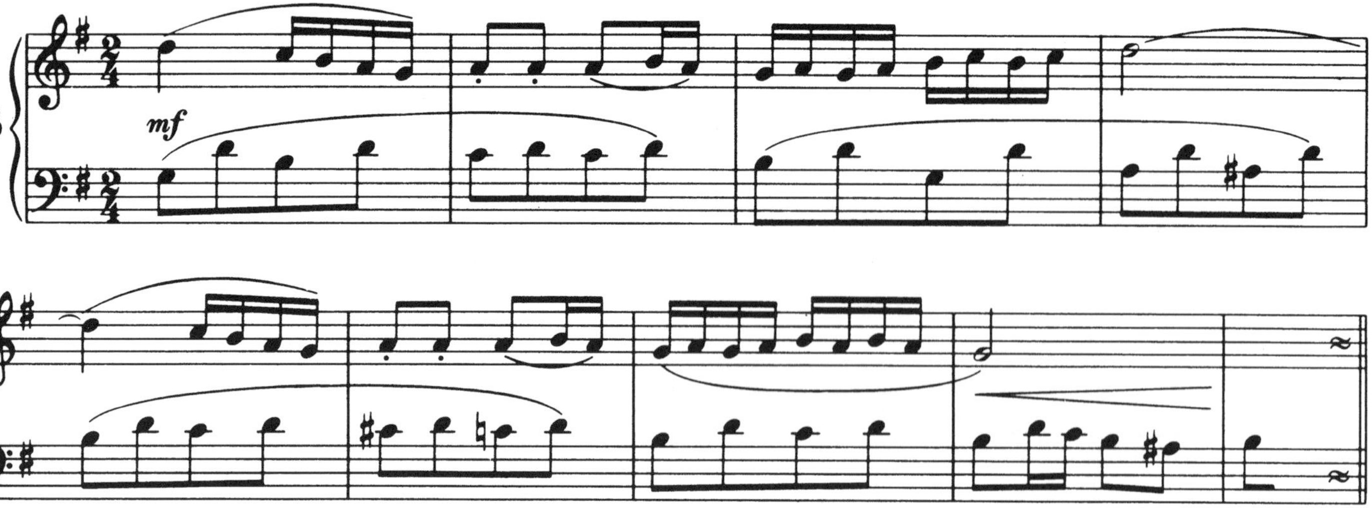

24

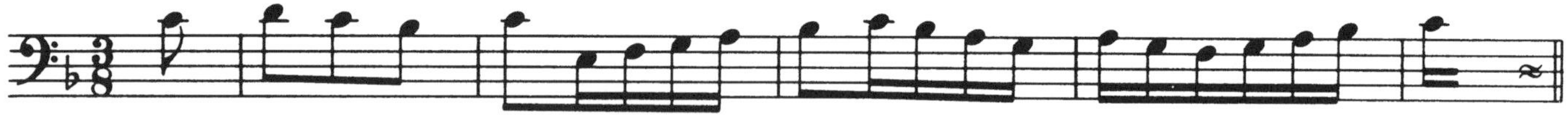

25

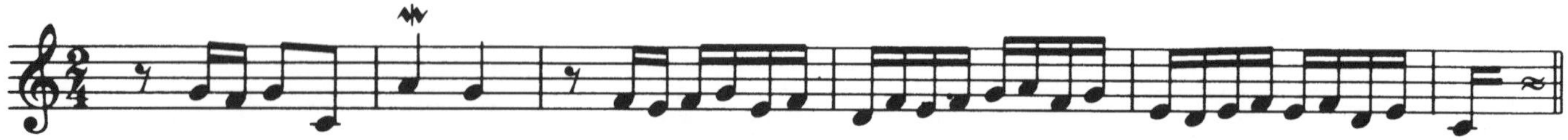

Lento maestoso 𝅗𝅥 = 54

26

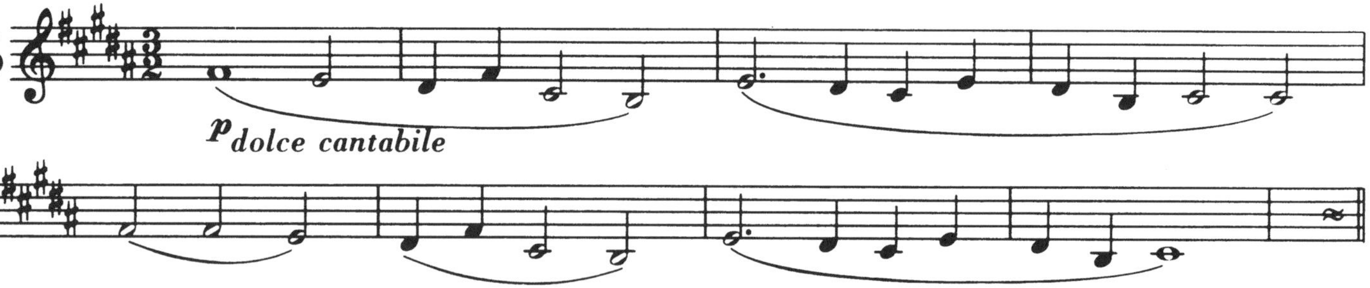

Examples 27 - 36 contain chromatically-altered notes within the span of five consecutive tones. The raising of the fourth degree of the scale is one of the most common alterations. This augmented fourth may be a fast neighbouring tone, such as the A in melody No. 27. But this alteration also can acquire greater importance by functioning as the leading tone to the dominant key. In such cases it then is heard as a new tonic of shorter or longer duration. This is known as a transitory (or passing) modulation. (Refer to Keyboard Harmony Exercise No. 26 and those immediately following.) When a definite key change takes place, we speak of firm modulation. As a rule, raised notes act as leading tones to the note a half step above.

The lowered note which we notice chiefly at the moment is the flatted sixth (submediant). It has a tendency to go downwards to the fifth degree of the scale, the dominant. See examples Nos. 28 and 29. (Refer also to Keyboard Harmony Exercise No. 26.)

Menuetto Trio

32

33

Ti par - ti, cor mio ca - ro, Mi las - s'in pian - t'a - ma - ro

E sen - z'al cun ri - pa - - ro L'a - ni - ma sen - za

te. Non ti par-tir da me Deh, cor mio ca-ro, Per le tua fè!

In examples Nos. 35 and 36 we encountered alterations of the first and fifth degrees of the scale. Presumably they caused no difficulty since the melodic movement proceeds step-wise.

The following examples use difficult leaps in approaching the augmented first and second degrees of the scale. Always try to imagine the note of resolution (the goal of the augmented note) before singing the chromatically altered note.

In example No. 37 therefore, first think [music] and then [music] and [music]

If you find examples Nos. 37 and 38 too difficult, leave them for the time being and return to them later.

37 [music]
Sü - - - ßer Freund, du bli-ckest mich ver-wun-dert an, kannst es nicht be-grei-fen, wie ich wei-nen kann; laß der feuch-ten Per - len un - ge-wohn -te Zier freu - dig hell er - zit - tern in dem Au - ge mir!

38 Adagio molto (♪ = 84) [music]

You may study example No. 38 (and similar examples) in the following ways:

(1) Sing the rhythm on one tone with a steady eight note pulse.

(2) Sing the tones of the melody in equal time values and in any comfortable octave. Slowly!

(3) Sing the melody as notated, but without the trills.

(4) Play the melody on an instrument with the trills, accents, dynamics, etc.

39 [music]
Hie und · da ist an den Bäu - men man - ches bun - te Blatt zu seh'n,

XI. Five-tone scale in minor with neighboring tones

Two important exercises:

1) Play and sing the minor versions of the harmonizations in Chapter X, page 37.
2) Practice minor triads carefully in the same way as you practiced major triads in Chapter IX, pages 33 and 34.

6. Som stjärnan uppå himmelen så klar hon längtar till sitt rum,
så längtar jag till dig, min lilla vän, var timme och var stund.
Var timme är som en månad lång, var månad som ett år.
Så längtar jag till dig, min lilla vän, fast jag dig aldrig får.

8. Appellon nau Le doux aigneau, Appellon nau, Appellon

nau, Le doux ai - gneau, si haut qu'il nous a - pe - - - re.

15. Li - mu, li - mu, li - ma, Gud låt so - len ski - na ö - ver ber - gen de blå, ö - ver kul - lor - na små som i sko - gen skall gå om somma - ren.

25. Så går en dag än från vår tid och kommer icke mer, och än en natt med Herrens frid till jorden sänkes ned.

Adagio

26. Ein-ge-schla-fen auf der Lau-er o-ben ist der al-te Rit-ter, drü-ben ge-hen Re-gen-schau-er und der Wald rauscht durch das Git-ter.

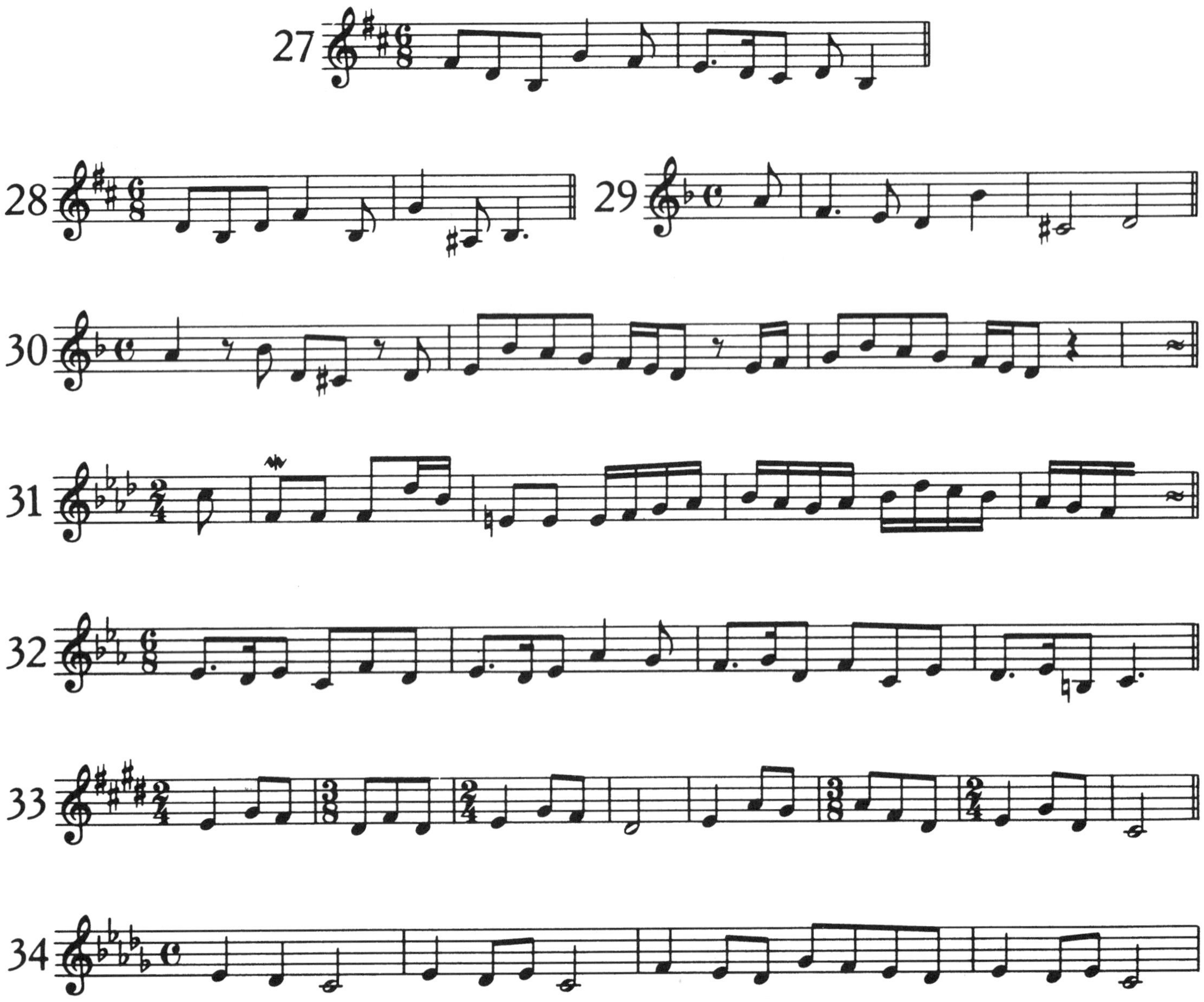
27
28
29
30
31
32
33
34

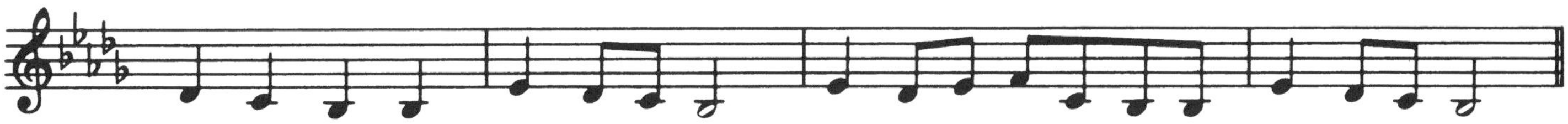

35

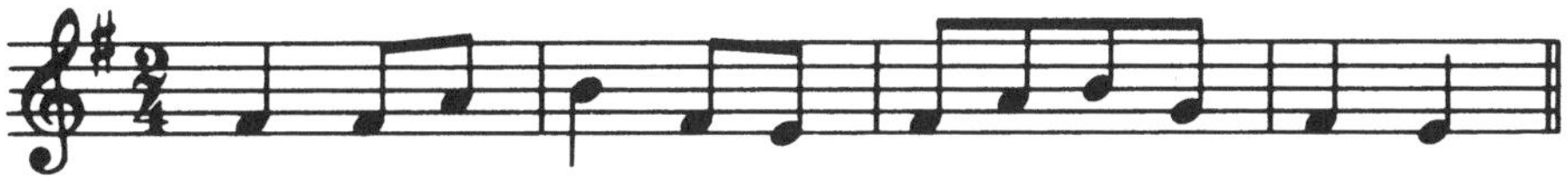

36

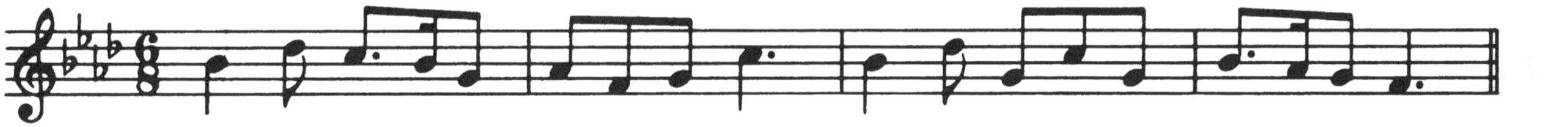

37

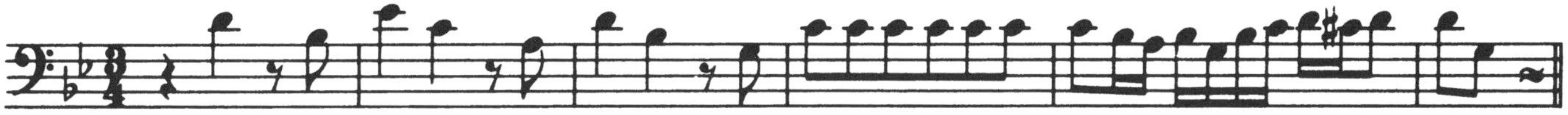

38

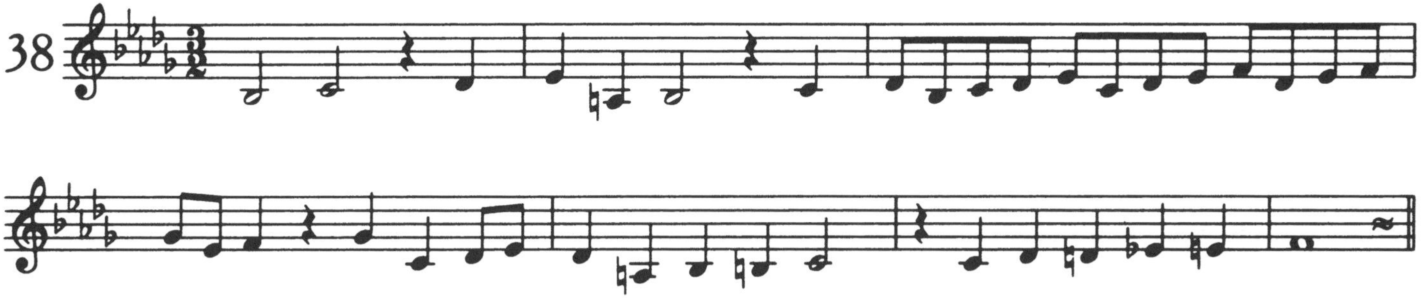

39

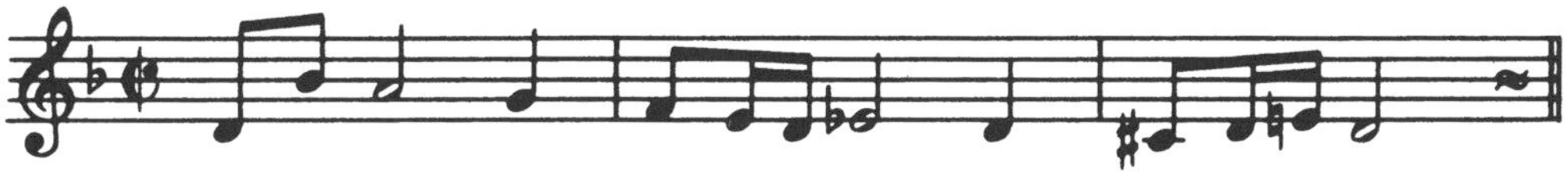

40 Was ver-meid ich denn die We - ge, wo die an-dern Wandrer gehn, su-che mir versteck-te Ste - ge durch ver-schnei-te Fel-sen-höhn? su-che mir versteck-te Ste - ge durch verschnei - te Fel-sen-höhn, durch Fel-sen-höhn?

41

Use the chordal material in Keyboard Harmony Exercises Nos. 1 - 25 in as many ways as possible.

In the following melodies the lower neighboring tone of the tonic lies a whole step below. Therefore if D is the tonic, we have:

This is the central group of notes in one of the old church modes - the Dorian plagal or Hypodorian (church mode II). Later several examples of diatonic melodies which are not governed by the tonal cadences and therefore are not related to major/minor tonality will be found. But first here are some simple examples in the Dorian mode:

42 Värl-dens Fräl-sa-re, kom här, re-na jung-frun mo-der är, ty en börd så un - der - lig, Her - re Je - su, höv - des dig.

43. Förlän oss Gud, i nåd, frid i vå - ra da - gar; ty in - gen är på jor - de - rik, _____ som o - frid kan för - ta - ga, u - tan du, Gud, al - le - na.

44. O Kris - te, du som lju - set är, dig kan ej mör - ker bli - va när.
Vi skå - da upp i tron till dig, när so - lens ljus för - döl - jer sig.

45. (3 times) (3 times)
Ky - ri - e e - - - le - i - son. Chri - ste _____ e - - - le - i - son.
(2 times)
Ky - ri - e e - - - le - i - son. Ky - ri - e _____ e - - - le - i - son.

Some old French carols:

46. Je me suis le-vé par un ma-ti-net Que l'au-be pre-nait Son blanc mante-let. Chantons no-let, no-let, no-let, chantons no-let en-co-re.

47. Al-lons, suivons, les Ma-ges, Qui char-gés de pré-sents Vont rend-re leurs hom-ma-ges A ce di-vin en-fant. Mais le meil-leur Est qu'ils don-nent leur coeur Un coeur ar-dent Est tout ce qu'il at-tend.

48. Or vous tremous-sez, pasteur de Ju-dé-e, Es-tes-vous las-sez i-quet-te ne-te-e. Chan-tez par-mi le pre-au Nau-let, nau-let, nau-let, nau

Chan - tez par - mi le pre - au Nau - let, nau - let, nau - let, nau Nau - let, nau - let, nau - let nau.

49 Voi-ci le jour de la nais-san - ce du fils de Dieu. En si-gne de ré-jou-is-san - ce dans ce saint lieu. Chantons d'un air mé-lo-di-eux quel - - que can-ti-que Qui plai-se au mo-narque des cieux Par sa dou-ce mu-si - - que.

The tonality of the church modes is made up largely of certain typical melodic formulas which reveal much more about the mode in question than merely the arrangement of the notes. Notice the typical Hypodorian melodic formula in Examples Nos. 42 - 44.

The use of formulas is called the modal system. (Modus, plur. modi, is used, as is known, as an identification for the church scales.) Many folksongs are modal. (See Chapter XV).

Contemporary composers often have used church or folksong modes. Here are a few examples from the works of Igor Stravinsky:

50 ♩= 80
Dai - gne, dai - gne très ai - mab - le mère ent - rer dans not(re) chau - miè - re la ma - ri - euse ai - der;

51. ¹⁾ Un beau ru-ban bleu, un beau ru-ban rouge
Un _____ ru-ban rouge comme mes joues.

52. Daig-ne aimable mèr(e), daigne ent-rer dans la chaumièr(e), daig-ne nous ai-der les boucles à dé-fair(e), les boucl(es) du marié – Daigne dé-mê-ler les boucl' du bouclé – En-tre Mère dans la chau-mièr(e) daig-ne nous ai-der les boucles à défair(e).

53. Et vous père et mè-re bé-nis-sez votre en-fant

¹⁾ If the rhythm is too difficult to sing at first, sing notes of equal length until you can sing the rhythm as given. Return to this example when you can master the exercises in Rhythm Exercises on page 176.

qui s'ap - pro - che fiè - rement tou - te mu - rail - le renver - sant.

(♩ = 50)

54

♩ = 60

55

molto cant. ma non f

56

p cantabile

XII. Arpeggiated cadences

The following exercises are based on arpeggios (broken chords) belonging to the cadential material. Practice in the following way:

1) Read through each example and determine on what chords it is based. Play these chords on the piano (right hand only) while you sing the example. In Example No. 1 therefore, the following chords are played:

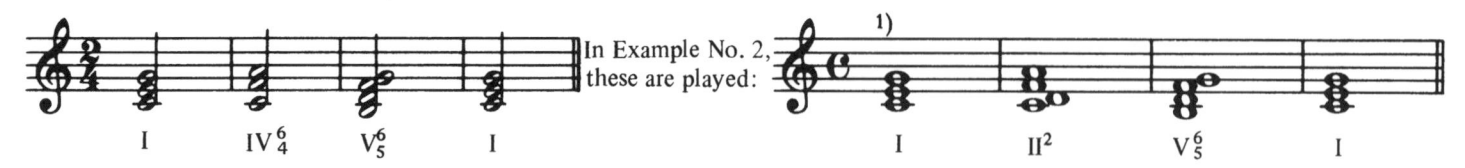

$$\text{I} \quad \text{IV}^6_4 \quad \text{V}^6_5 \quad \text{I} \qquad \text{In Example No. 2, these are played:} \qquad \text{I} \quad \text{II}^2 \quad \text{V}^6_5 \quad \text{I}$$

2) Sing the examples without using the piano. Always try to hear the chord notes sounding together as harmonic entities.

3) Practice the major examples in minor and vice-versa.

[1] Refer to Keyboard Harmony Exercise No. 18

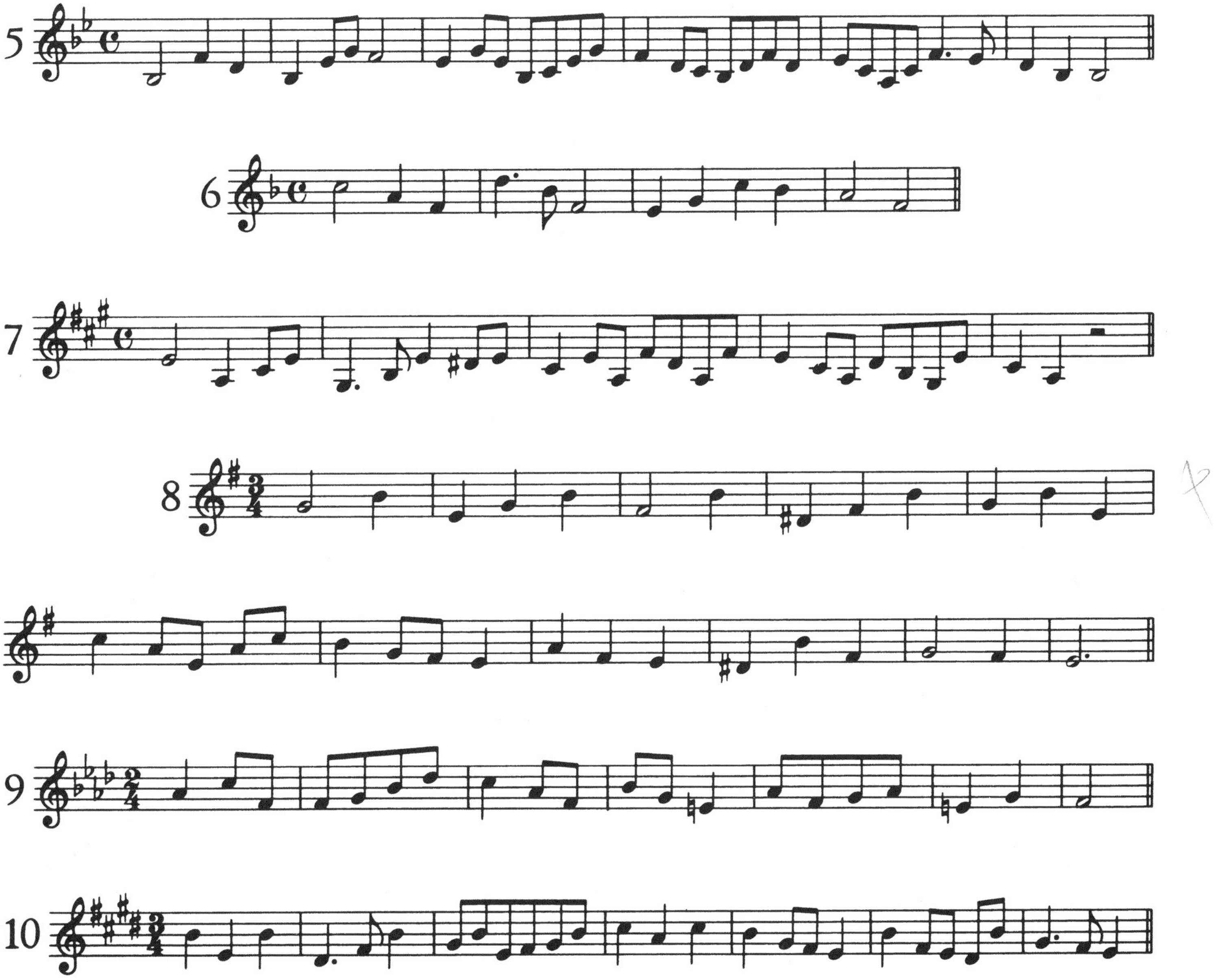
5
6
7
8
9
10

XIII. The major scale

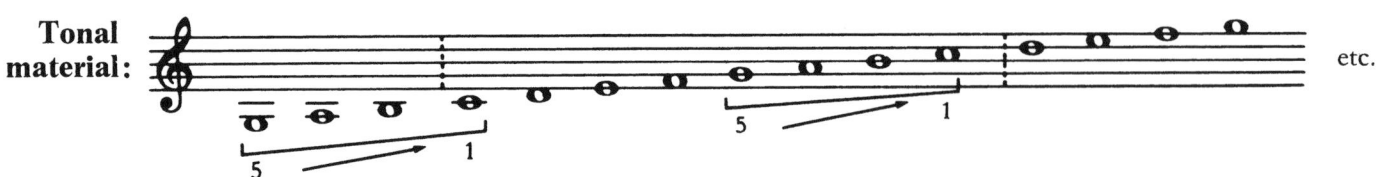

Tonal material: etc.

The step-wise movement from the dominant degree of the scale upwards to the tonic, forming a perfect fourth (5↗1, see group of notes above), should be practiced first by using the following simple harmonic exercise:

Exercise:
Play and sing this chord in all major keys, naming the notes.

I   V⁷   I

The group of notes given is a triad with the tonic doubled at the top:

This triad contains two new intervals. The interval formed by the third of the chord and the tonic above (3↗1) is a minor sixth.

If the triad is put in second inversion (with the fifth as the lowest note)

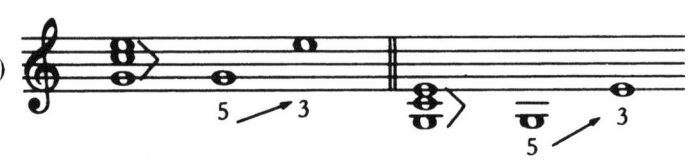

or into open position:

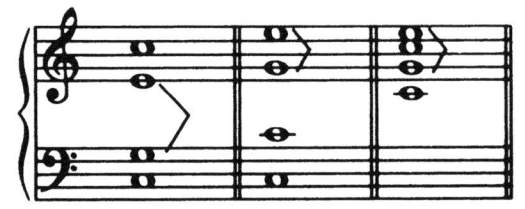

then the interval of a major sixth is formed from the fifth of the triad up to its third. (5 ↗ 3)

Exercise:

It is most important to practice the sixths in open positions of the triad. Play the triads in Chapter IX, part A, page 33, on the piano. Sing and name the notes of the major and minor sixths of each triad that result from the following progressions a) 5 ↗ 3   c) 3 ↗ 1
b) 3 ↘ 5   d) 1 ↘ 3

Be sure to read and sing upwards and downwards, beginning with all the notes in the chromatic scale (see Chapter VIII, page 31), the new intervals which you have encountered in Chapters X - XIII: Perfect fifth, diminished fifth, major sixth, and minor sixth.

Melodies

Allegro non troppo ma con brio

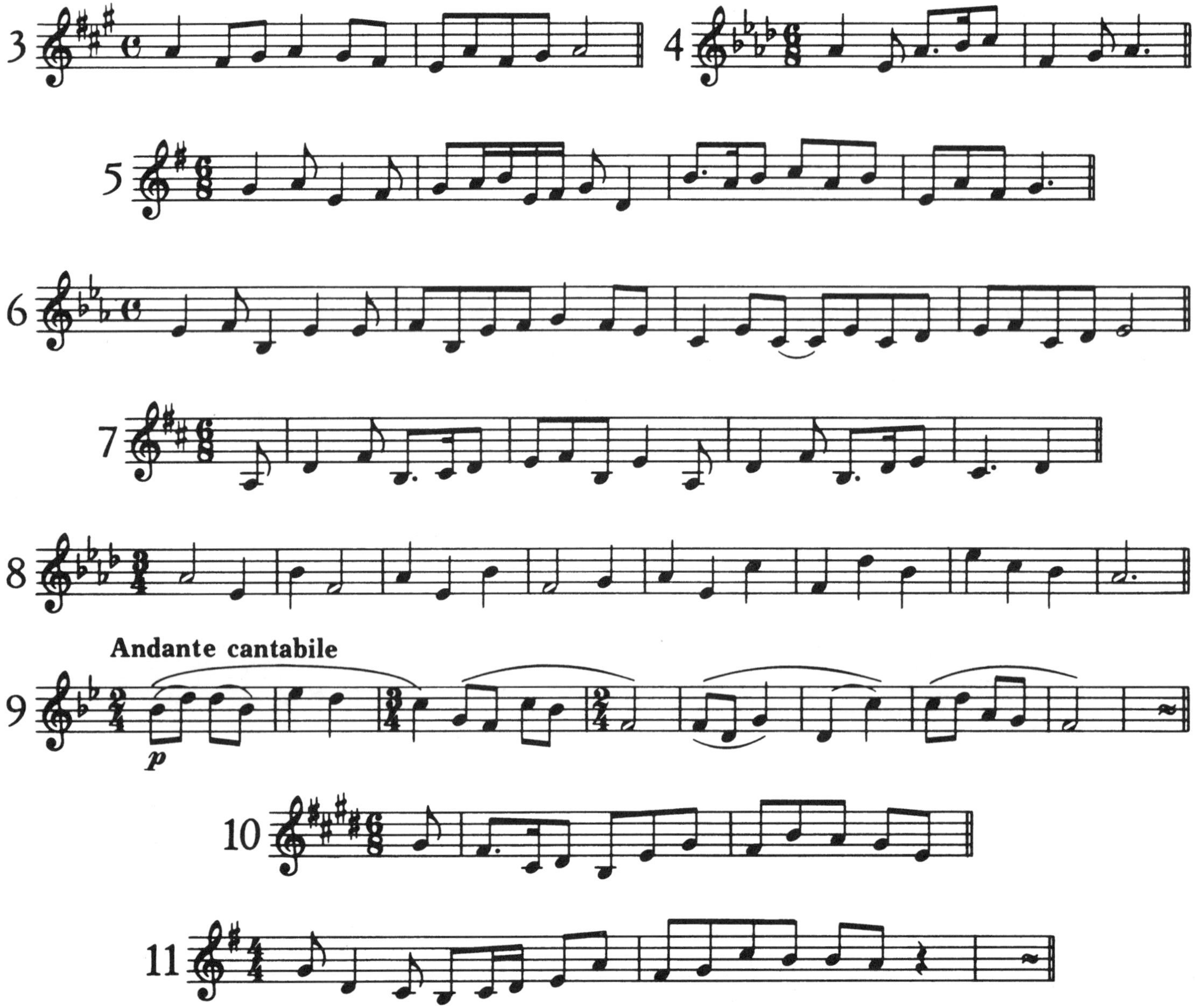
3
4
5
6
7
8
Andante cantabile
9
p
10
11

13. I had a little nuttree, nothing would it bear, but a silver nut-meg, and a golden pear. The King of Spain's daughter came to vi-sit me, and all for the sake of my little nut-tree.

14. Ein Jüng-ling liebt ein Mäd-chen, die hat ei-nen An-dern er-wählt; der And're liebt ei-ne And're, und hat sich mit die-ser ver-mählt.

Andante larghetto

15. Their sound is gone out, their sound is gone out in-to all lands. in-to all lands.

66

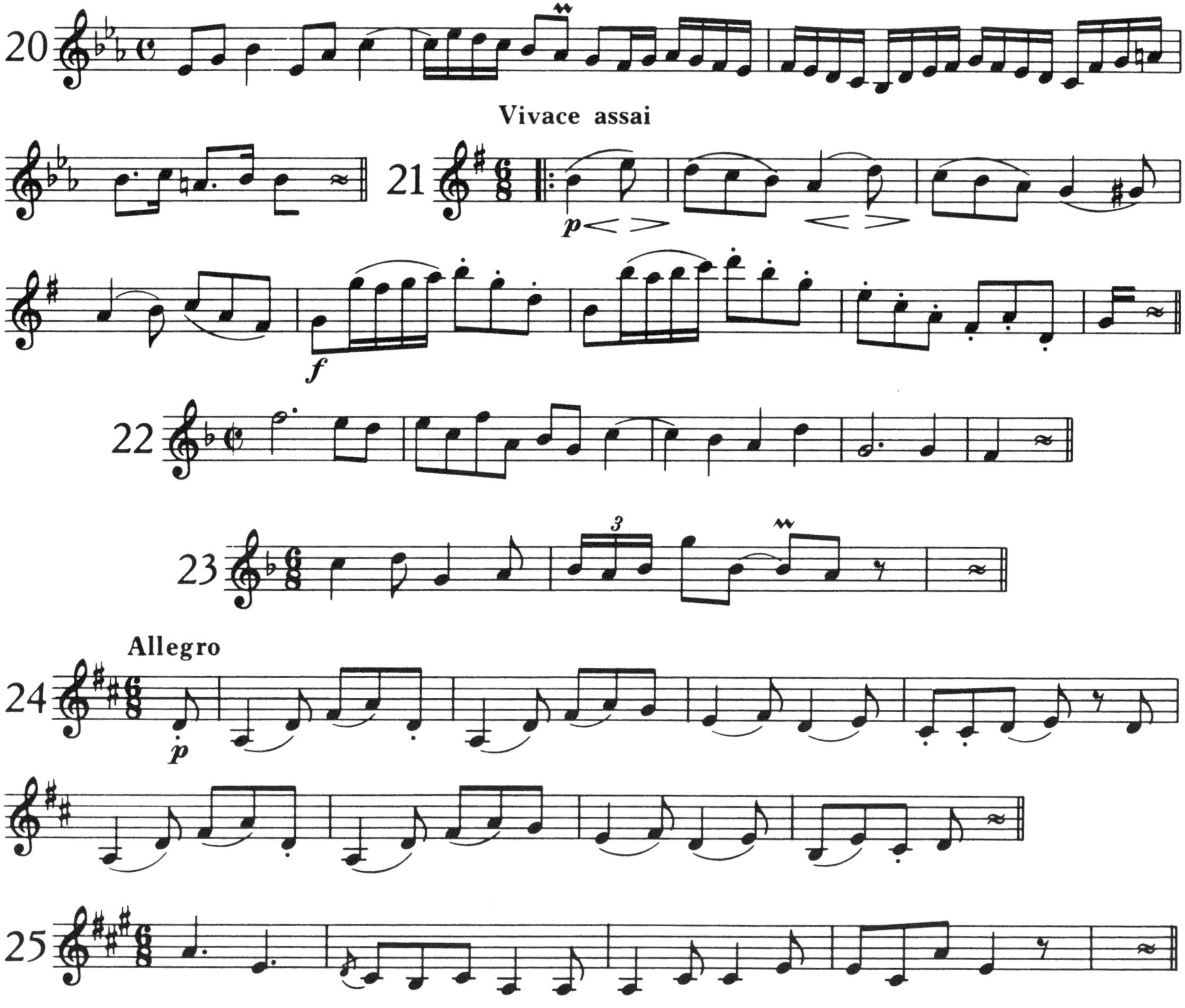
20
Vivace assai
21
22
23
Allegro
24
25

Allegro

26

27 I saw a ship a-sai-ling, a-sai-ling on the sea. And Oh! it was a-laden with pret-ty things for me. There was com-fits in the ca-bin and apples in the hold. The sails were made of sa-tin, and the mast was made of gold.

28 Vin-den drar, skeppet far bort till fjär-ran land. Och sjö-mans-gos-sens lil-la, lil-la vän står sör-jan-de på strand.

29 Nej, fåfängt'. Vart jag ser, ej min-sta nymf ger ö-gat ro, om

ej i grus och ler en klack-lapp av en sko.

Ej vi-sar mig en täck ber-gère sin fot i språn-get blyg.
Vad ser jag? Toffeln lig-ger där för-u-tan ö-ver-tyg.

Brisk and happy

30.

31. Det bod-de en fru allt Sö-der un-der Ö, hon ha-de en dot-ter som kal-la-des Mal-fred. Den Sjön han gror al-drig.

32. Jungfru Mar-jo hon skul-le åt af-ton-sång-en gån-ga. Tiden görs mig lång. Så gick hon den vä-gen åt ber-get låg. Herren Gud vet sorgen den är tung.

33. Och lil-la Ka-rin tjän-te på ko-nungens gård. Hon tjän-te där så län-ge u-ti tolv he-la år. U-ti ro-sen.

34. *Allegretto* — *p* — *sfp* — *sfp*

35. *Allegro teneramente* — *sempre p e dolce*

71

Allegro con brio

36

Allegro moderato

37

Andante

40

As when the dove laments her love, All on the naked spray.

41

Mein teu - rer Heiland, laß dich fra - gen, laß dich fra - gen, teu - rer

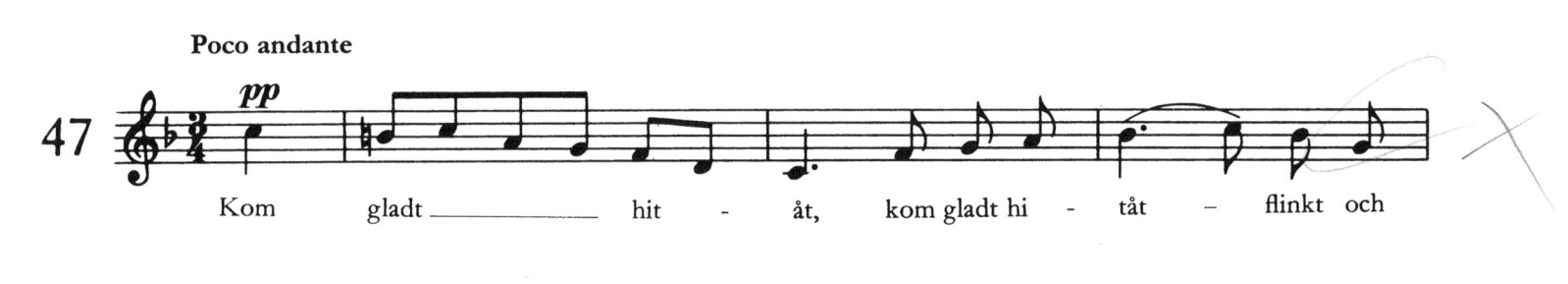

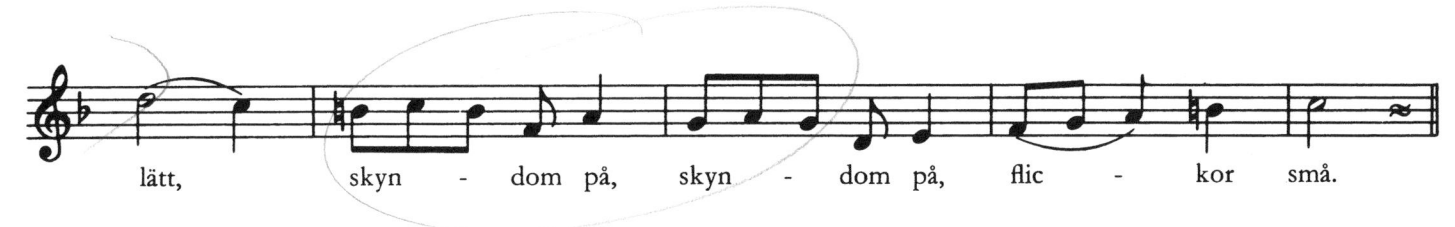

Hei - land, laß dich fra - gen, laß dich fra - gen, teu-rer Hei-land, laß dich fragen:

Poco andante

47 Kom gladt hit - åt, kom gladt hi - tåt — flinkt och lätt, skyn - dom på, skyn - dom på, flic - kor små.

48 Kom hit och välj och köp, se här, de blom - mor vår - en skö - nast bär! Kom, va - let gör er ej be -

74

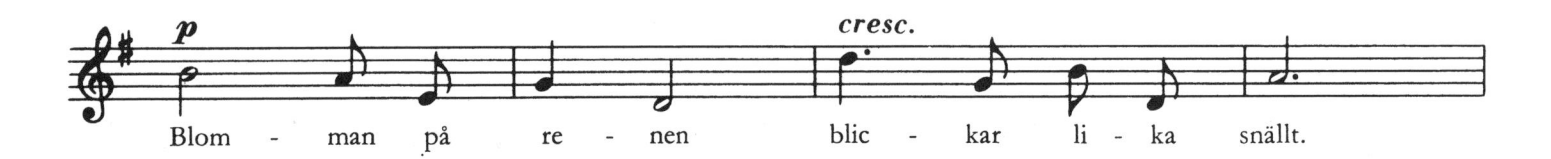

svär, jag har de bäs - ta qvar, de bäs - ta qvar.

49 **Poco allegretto**

Få - geln på gre - nen sjun - ger li - ka gällt.

p   *cresc.*

Blom - man på re - nen blic - kar li - ka snällt.

mf   *mf*

Men allt - se - dan dig jag såg har för - änd - rats all min håg.

p

He - la da - gen jag be - ta - gen ser och hör blott dig.

In several of these exercises you may notice that it is easy to use the parallel triads of the major key (submediant, supertonic, mediant). This may be practiced in Keyboard Harmony Exercise No. 38. It also may be meaningful to do this exercise in connection with the harmonization of melodies in that chapter.

Recitatives often provide excellent practice in reading a melody. The ability to read the Bach recitative below (and by reading we mean as always, not only the ability to hear it in your head, but also to sing it) depends on one's proficiency in reading the harmonic progressions. To a great extent the following melodies contain the notes of the chords indicated by the figured bass symbols. These numbers, written below the bass note, are a musical shorthand to indicate the desired interval(s) above the given bass note. Thus the examples also provide practical figured bass exercises using chords in conjunction with the Figured Bass Exercises beginning on page 179. If you have difficulty in finding the right note, you always should find the broken chord of which the "difficult" interval usually forms a part (see the inserted notes in parentheses in the first recitative).

A good method for singing recitatives is as follows:

(1) Play the figured bass part and sing each chord, naming the notes, while the piano is still sounding.

(2) Play the figured bass part and sing the recitative with or without the text.

(3) Sing the recitative without help from the piano.

If a student cannot play the piano, the figured bass part should be played by the teacher or some other person.

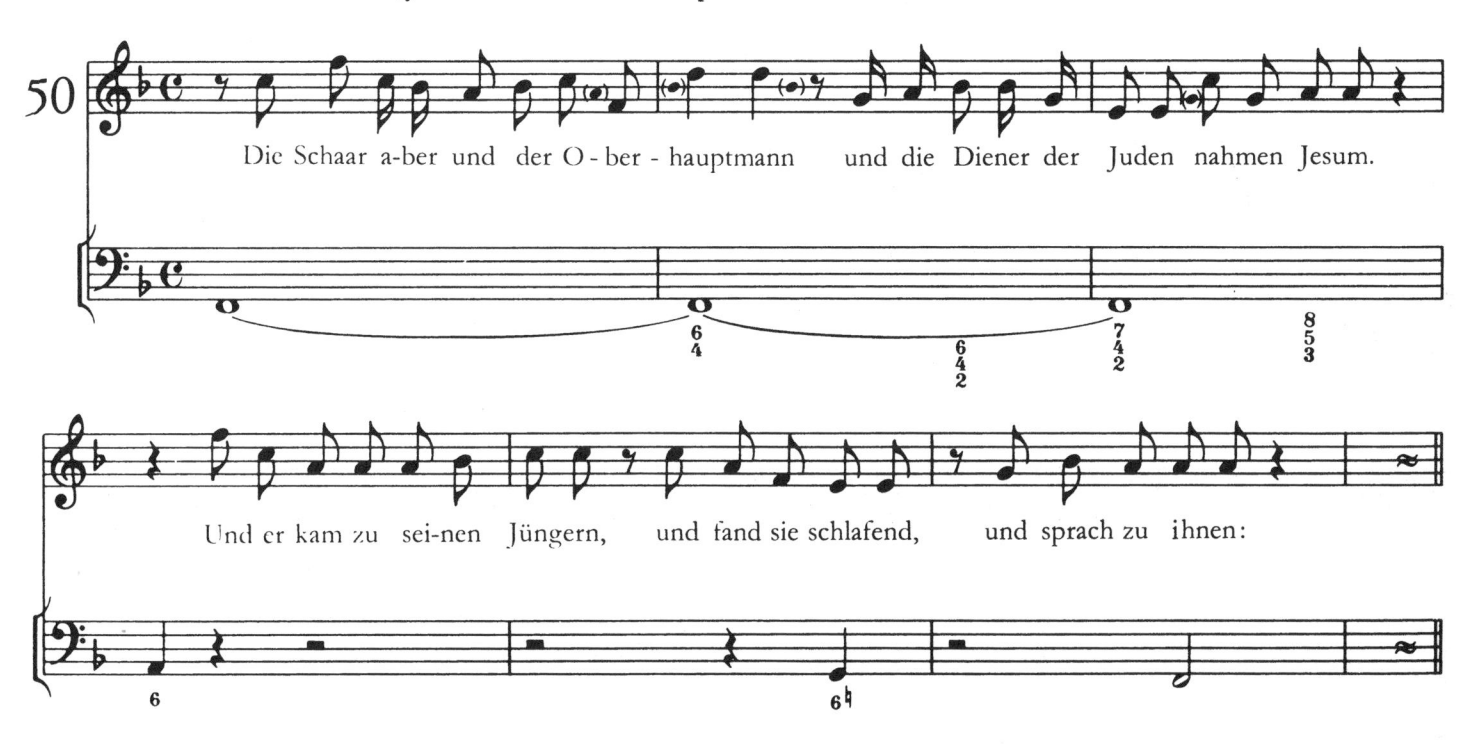

51. Da ging hin der Zwölfen einer, mit Namen Judas Ischarioth, zu den Hohenpriestern und sprach:

52. Gehet hin in die Stadt zu Einem, und sprecht zu ihm: Der Meister läßt dir sagen: Meine Zeit ist hier, ich will bei dir die Ostern

77

halten mit meinen Jüngern.

53 Evangelist: Da kam Jesus mit Ihnen zu einem Hofe, der hieß Gethsemane, und sprach zu seinen Jüngern:

Jesus: Setzet euch hier, bis daß ich dorthin gehe und bete.

Evangelist: Da Jesus diese Rede vollendet hatte, sprach er zu seinen Jüngern: Ihr wisset, daß nach zweien Tagen Ostern wird, und des Menschen Sohn wird überantwortet werden, daß er gekreuziget werde.

Evangelist: Da sprach Pilatus zu ihm: **Pilatus:** So bist du dennoch ein König? **Evangelist:** Jesus antwortete: **Jesus:** Du sagst's, ich bin ein König. Ich bin dazu geboren und in die Welt kommen, daß ich die Wahrheit zeugen soll. Wer aus der Wahrheit ist, der höret meine Stimme.

XIV. The minor scale

Tonal material

C minor

The relative minor of C major is A minor.

Those notes of the minor scale which lie between the tonic and the fifth (1↗5) differ only from the corresponding part of the major scale in the lowered third. The other part, from 5↗1, is more complex because the sixth and seventh degrees are variable, accounting for the different pitch sequences of the natural, harmonic, and melodic minor scales.

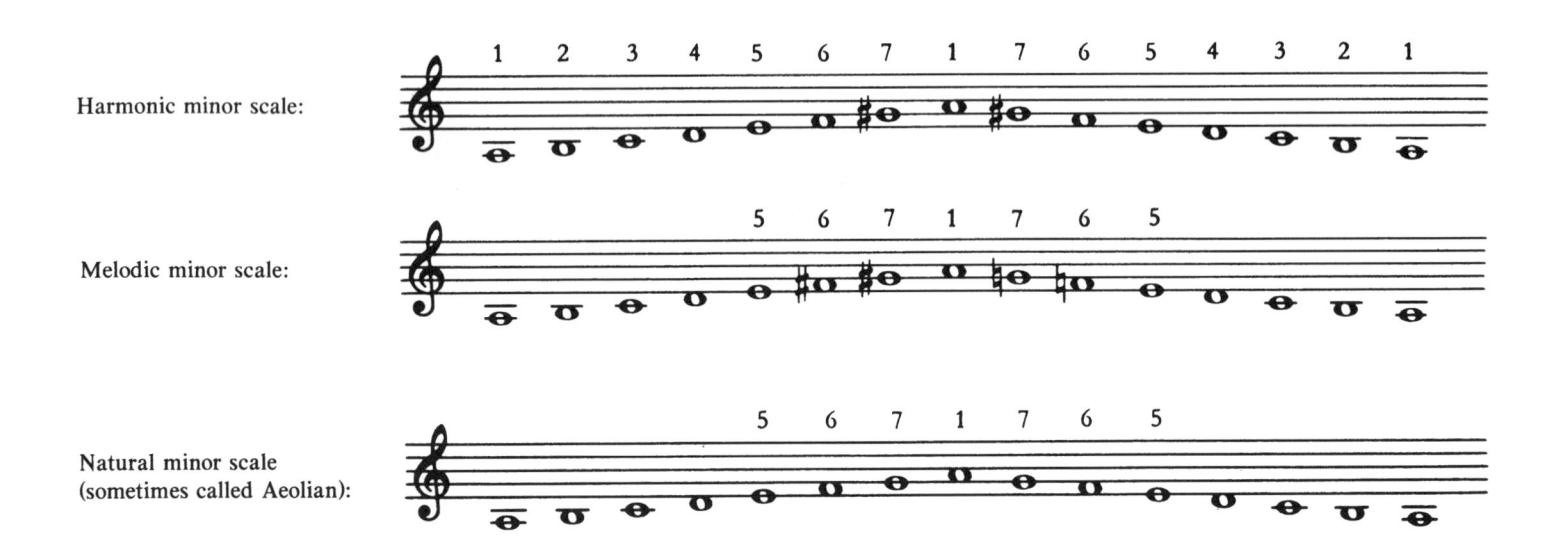

Harmonic minor scale:

Melodic minor scale:

Natural minor scale (sometimes called Aeolian):

Dorian scale:

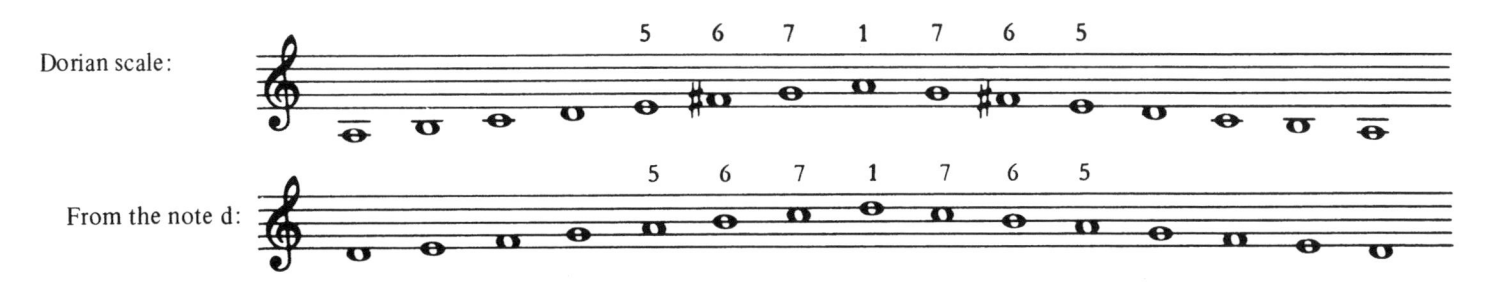

From the note d:

All scales are specific patterns of tones. They are foundations of total musical ideas - general basis for compositions. Melodies rarely confine themselves to a fixed scale pattern. To explain their differences we may examine them as follows:

Let us begin with the natural minor scale:

In a perfect cadence in a minor however, the third of the dominant is raised to g♯ in order to give the feeling of the leading tone rising to the tonic a:

If we arrange this particular group of notes into scale form, the result will be a harmonic minor scale. As you can see, this scale has an augmented second between the sixth and seventh degrees, or the submediant (which tends to fall) and the leading tone (which tends to rise).

In traditional Western melodies this augmented interval often has been considered difficult to sing and perhaps also ugly to hear, and therefore it has been avoided. Even today it sounds somewhat exotic, as in this excerpt from Geroges Bizet's opera, *Carmen:*

The augmented second does occur in several East European and non-European types of scales (see Chapter XV). In major/minor tonality it is common for the natural sixth and seventh degrees to be used in downward movement (stressing the direction towards the dominant), and the raised sixth and seventh degrees to be used in upward movement (stressing the direction towards the tonic). For example, in Carl Nielsen's song "Irmelin Rose":

Se, der var en gang en Kon - - ge, mangen Skat han kald - te sin.

The result is what we call the melodic minor scale.
The harmonization of the movement 5→1 with the raised sixth and seventh degrees can be written like this:

I   IV#   VII⁶   I

The Dorian key belongs to the medieval system of church modes - a subject not theoretically treated in this book (1). Here we shall restrict ourselves to a few observations on a typical Dorian melody taken from plainsong in order to illustrate the difference between the tonal material of the scale and the Dorian melodies themselves. The Dorian repertoire used is monophonic. In modal polyphony, however, additional factors apply.

*Ro - ra - te coe - - - li de - su - - - - per,
et nu - bes plu - rant ju - - - - stum: ap - pe - ri - a - - - tur ter - ra,*

(1) Chapter XV however does contain some melodic material for practice in melody reading.
(2) The sign ⌇⌇ (quilisma) is a performance practice sign. The line indicates a somewhat lengthened tone and ⌇ a short and somewhat voiceless one.

[musical notation: et ger-mi-net Sal-va-to-rem.]

Some observations:
1) The tonic (usually called the finalis) is d.
2) Both the raised and the lowered sixths, b♮ and b♭, occur. In each instance the lowered sixth, b♭, appears as a note falling to the dominant a. The raised sixth, b♮, appears to rise as a link between the dominant a and the leading tone c.
3) Tonally, the c is a very important note (see the word desuper) and in turn is related closely to the fifth below, f. Melodically, the c plays a more important role than the high d (the tonic), which here is only a "neighboring tone" to the c. The melody therefore encompasses a range of c^1–c^2, rather than d^1–d^2.

Melodies:

Allegretto (Polska)

(11)

(12)

Adagio

(13)

85

Allegro

14

15

Etwas langsam

16

Ei - ne Krä - he war mit mir aus der Stadt ge - zo - gen.

Mässig

17

Nun merk' ich erst, wie müd' ich bin, da ich zur Ruh mich le - ge;

18

Ro - sa lil - la tal - te till sin Bro - der så Under linden Hvad spor - de du för nytt up - på tin - get i går Så sent om en af - tons ti - der.

Andante

19

20 Hertig Hil - le-brand han ri - der på ri - ka Grefvens gård U - ti lunden. Och ri - ka Grefvens dot - ter för honom u - te står. Den jag hafver tingat i min ungdom.

Allegro appassionato

21 *espress.* *cresc.*

22 He trusted in God that he would de - li - ver him; let him de - li - ver him, if he de-light in him

23 Och hör du lil - la båtsman Hvad jag nu sä - ger dig. Och vil - le du nu spe - la gull - tär - ning med mig? De spe - la - de, de spe - la - de gull - tärning.

24. Jag gack mig ut en midsommardag, då grödan och örterna gror.

Det var två ädela konungabarn, de lofde hvarandra sin tro.

25. "Og hør Hr. Peder! Bliv hjemme i Aar! du ved ej, hvad jeg i min Ungdom er spaad." I men Søen drager under.

26. Rosa lilla tjente på Konungens gård med äran och med dygd. Och der tjente hon uti åtta runda år. I vinnen väl, I vinnen väl både Rosor och Liljor.

27. Och Wal-le-mo han sad-la-de gån-gar-en grå U-ti löndom. Så red han sig till jungfru Hil-debrands gård. För detta var mig timat i min ungdom.

28. Det var den lil-la Ka-rin som tjen-te på Konung-ens gård. Hon tjen-te bland de lil-jor och bland de ro-sor små.

Sarabande

29.

Moderato

30. *p*

Allegretto (♩ = 138)

31. *f*

89

90

36.

37. Det lig-ger ett slott i Ö-ster-rik, Det lig-ger så väl be-bun-det Med sil-ver och det rö-da gull, rö-da gull, Med mar-mor-ste-nar upp-mu-rat.

38.

39.

40.

41.

Allegro vivace

44. Om al-la berg och da-lar vo-ro vän-da u-ti guld, Allt vat-ten vo-re vändt u-ti vin; Allt-sammans vill' jag vå-ga för dig min lil-la vän, Om du vor' all-ra-kä-re-stan min.

45. Det bod - de en fru på Tros - se - ri - ka ö; Hon ha - de en dot - ter som het - te Mal - fred; Den sor - gen gror ald - rig.

46. Sjun - ger jag, så hör du mig; Grå - ter jag, så rör det dig.

47.

48.

Adagio

49.

50.

In several of these exercises it may be easy to exchange the parallel chords of major and minor keys. This may be practiced in Keyboard Harmony Exercises Nos. 38 and 39. It also may be helpful to work with these exercises in connection with melodic harmonization, since we now have completed the chapter on melodies. Examples Nos. 26 - 32 (-37) as well as 40 - 43 in the Keyboard Harmony Exercises will provide an even greater variety for harmonization.

XV. Melodies not in major/minor tonality

This chapter deals with a number of melodies whose tonality in many cases is not major/minor. Most of the examples are in some type of mode (see pages 57 and 82).

In reading almost any melody one must be aware of tonality as well as the intervals. The same applies here. The student therefore is advised not to sing using the "one interval at a time" principle. He must imagine whole shapes. It is now, just as before, a question of melodic studies, not intervallic exercises. Before singing a melody, the student is advised to determine the tonic. This will make it easier for him to become aware of the special types of tonality encountered here.

Otherwise the melodies are stated without comment. A perceptive teacher will be able to find numerous examples illustrating the treatment of different tonal systems and types of scales.

Sources of the melodies can be found on page 204

1

May - en - zeit o - ne neidt freu - den geit wi - der - streit, sein
Uff dem Plan o - ne wan sicht man stan wol - ge - tan,

wi - der - ku - mer han uns al - len hel - ffen. Durch das gras sind
Lich - te präu - ne plüm - lein bay den gel - ffen.

sie schon uf ge - drun - gen und der walt ma - nig - vald un - get - zalt

ist der - schalt. Das er ward mit dem nie bas ge - sun - gen.

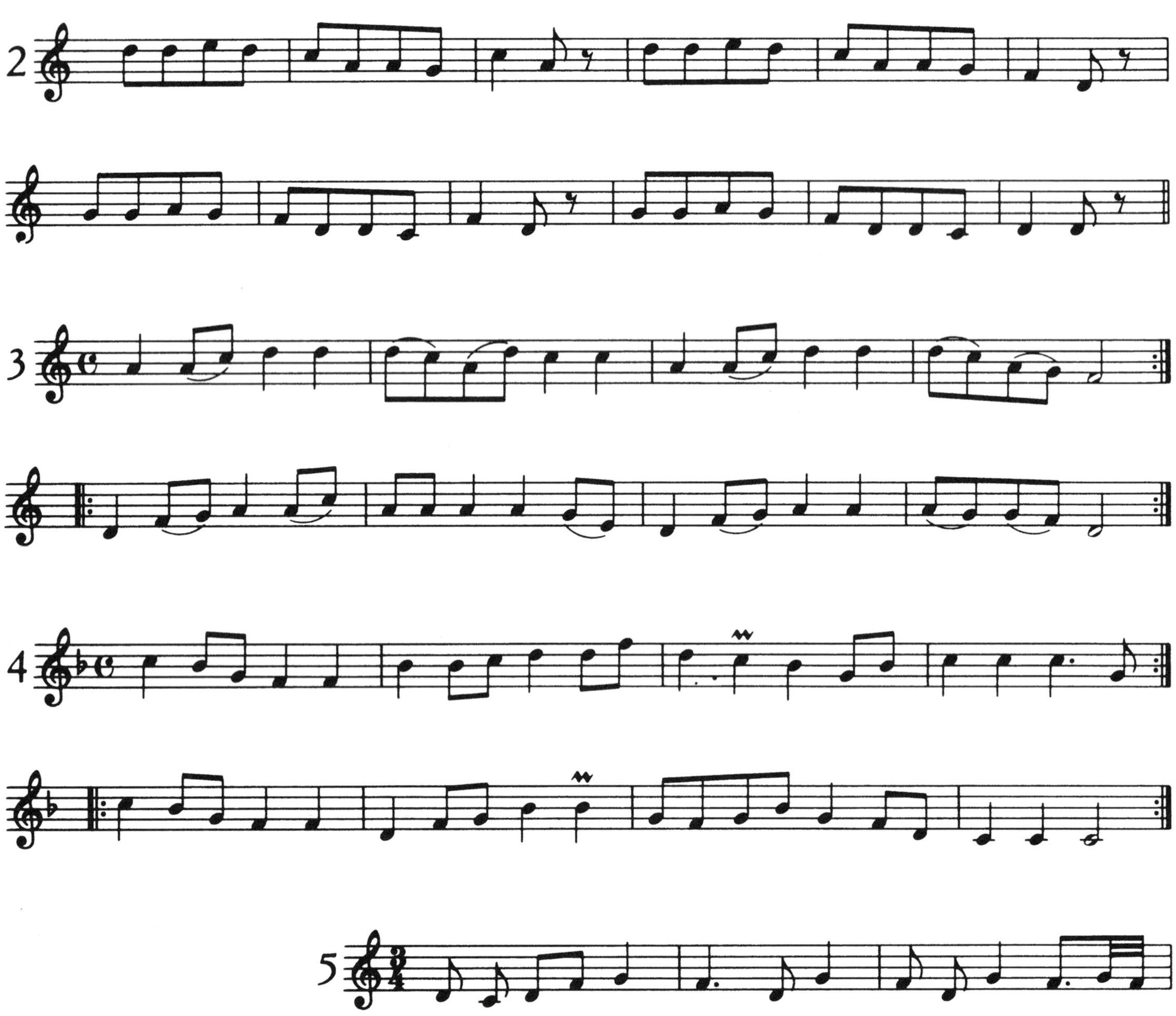

95

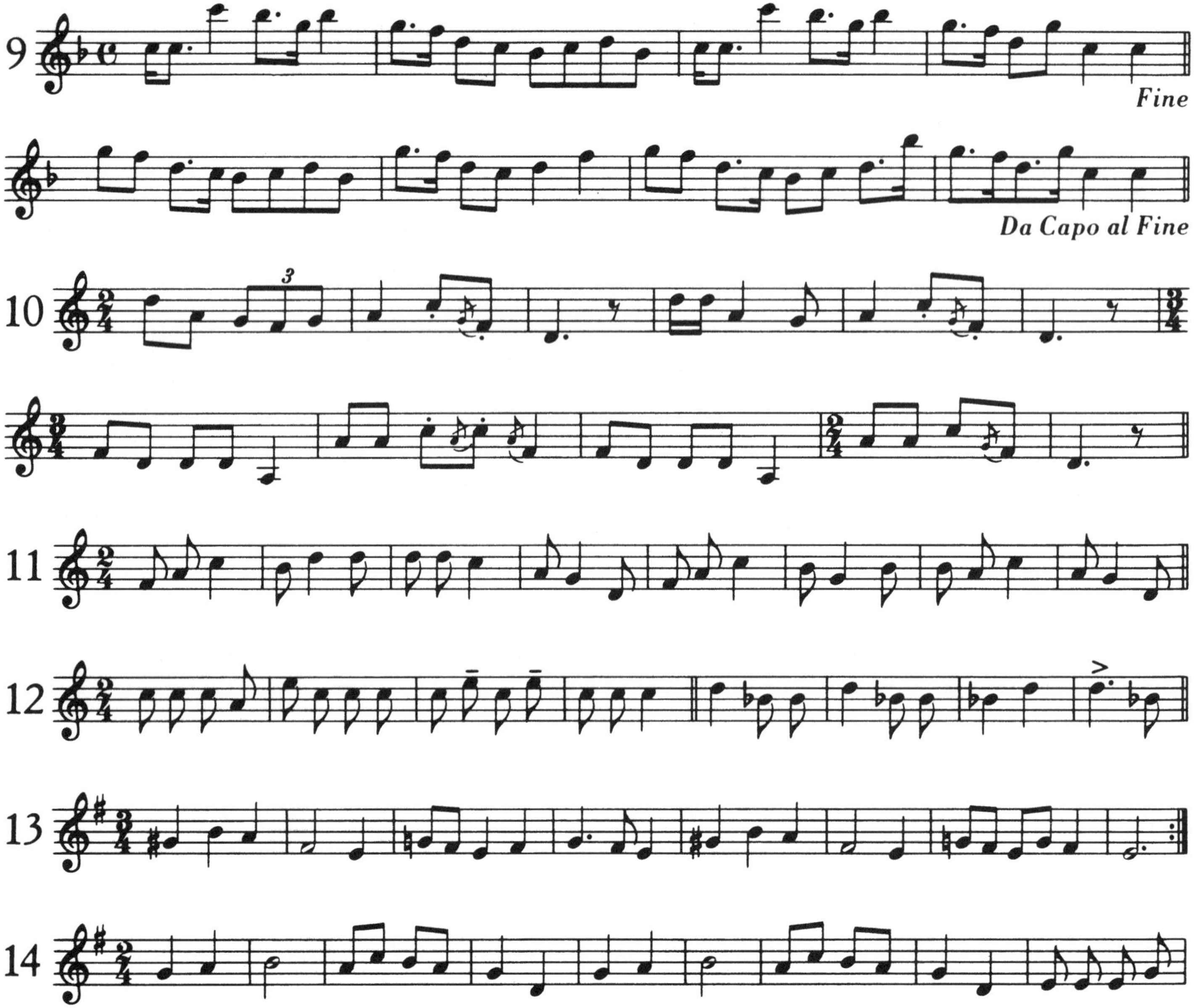
9
Fine
Da Capo al Fine
10
3
11
12
13
14

15.

1. U-na ma-ti-na-da fres-ca, vaig sor-tir per' na ca-car, no'n tro-bo per-diu ni guat-lla per a po-der-li ti-rá.
2. Si no u-na po-bra pa-sto-ra que'n guar-da-va el be-stia. Ja l'en tro-bo a-dor-mi-de-ta a la vo-ra d'un can-yar.
3. De tant bo-ni-que-ta qu'e-ra no la'n go-so des-per-tar, ne cu-llo un pom de vio-las y al-pit le ni vaig ti-rar.

1.-3. Si'm ti-ra l'a-mór y'm to-ca, si'm to-ca be'm to-ca-rá.

19. Luullahan, jotta on lysti olla, kun minä aina laulan.
Laululla ni minä pienet surut sydämeni pohjaan painan.
Laululla ni minä pienet surut sydämeni pohjaan painan.

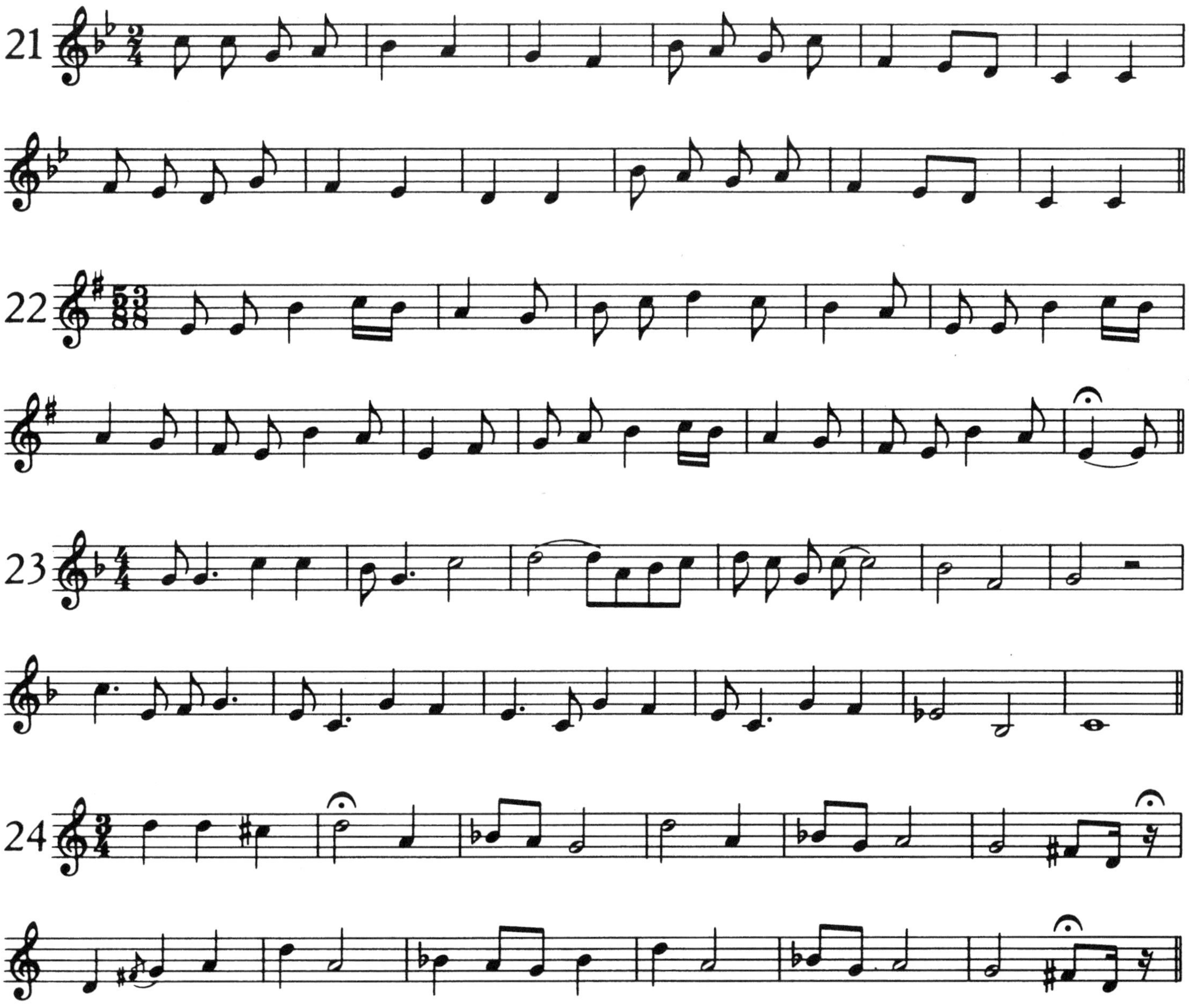
21
22
23
24

26.
Ca' the ewes to the knowes, 'ca them whaur the hea-ther grows.

Ca' them whaur the burn-ie rows my bon-nie dear-ie.

1. Hark, the ma-vis' ev'-nin' sang, sound-ing Clu-den's woods a-mang;
2. We'll gae down by Clu-den' side, thro' the ha-zels spread-ing wide,
3. Fair and love-ly as thou art, thou hast stown my ve-ry heart:

then a-fauld-in' let us gang, my bon-nie dear-ie.
o'er the waves that sweet-ly glide to the moon sae cleut-ly.
I can die, but can-na part, my bon-nie dear-ie.

29. Al-men Ah-tje, dat gaik-viek-sak gen gul fa-mon gaik ver-alt le;
dat le ai nåu un-ne juh-ko na-to, mav gul dat gaik-viek-sak jår-rå-tal-la ja gieht-ja-ta,
vo-lo, vo-lo, vo-lo, vo-lo, vo-lo, vo-lo, vo-lo, vo-lo, vo-lo, vo-lo, vo-lo, vo-lo.

31. Få-ra-her-de, få-ra-her-de, tra-la-la-la-lej, vill du in-te flyt-ta di-na får och lamm till mej? Få-ra-her-de, få-ra-her-de om till mej du går, skall du all-tid fin-na saf-tigt gräs för di-na får.

32.

33.

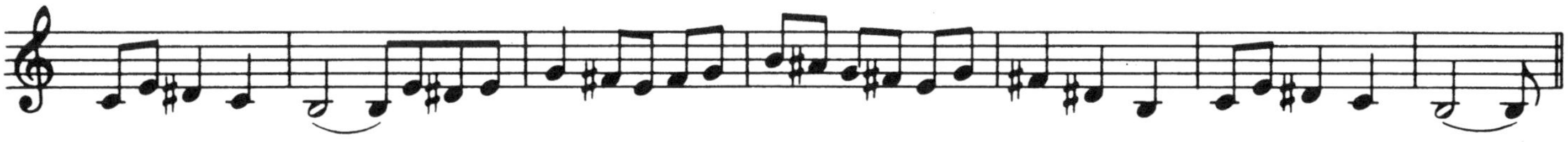

34

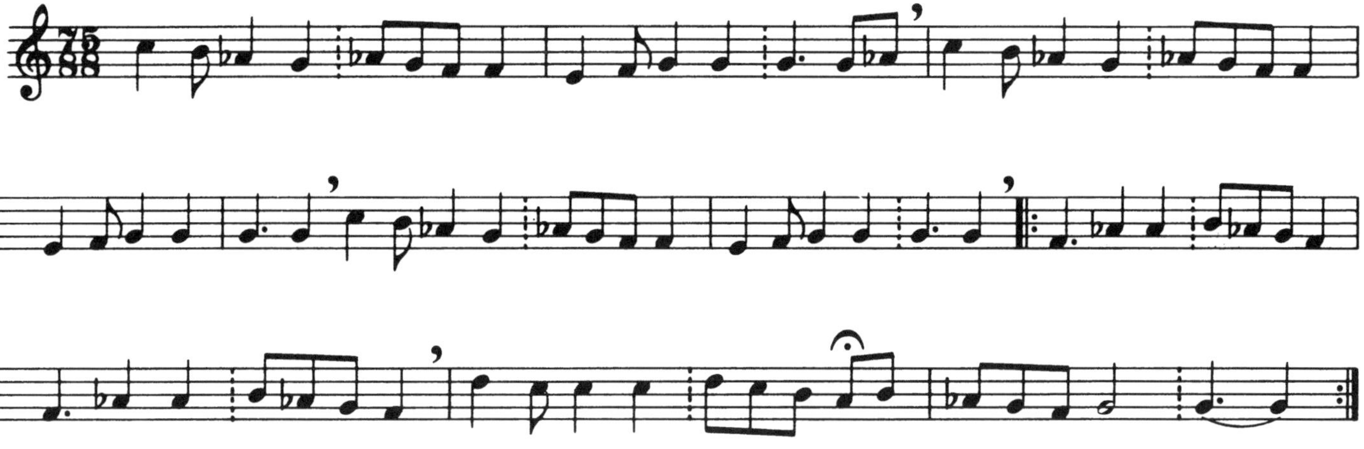

35

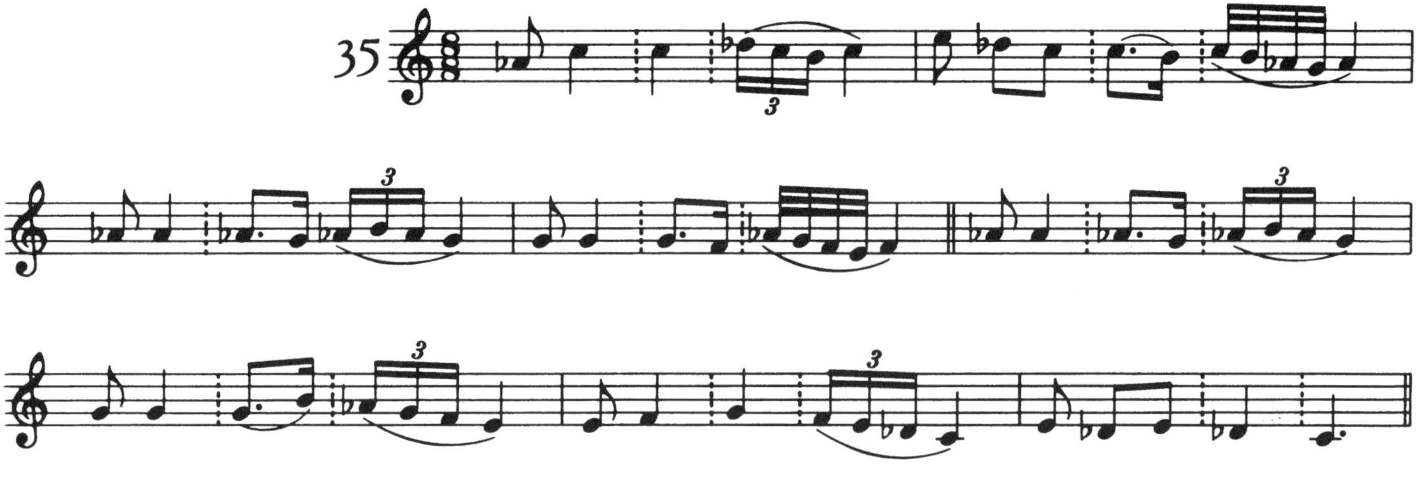

XVI. The dominant seventh chord

We have stressed previously the importance of focusing attention on whole groups of notes or shapes when reading melodies. These shapes have generally consisted of triads.

Now study the melodic line in the following excerpt from the St. Matthew Passion by J.S. Bach:

As you see, the melody is governed by two V^7 chords: In the first bar the V^7 on e♭ and in the second the V^7 on c (in spite of the fact that the figured bass has an e, which simply means the chord is used in first inversion). You will find it much easier to sing the minor sevenths of the melody e♭→1♭ and c→b♭ if you can hear the chords of which the sevenths are a part - that is, think of the V^7 chords in all of bar 1 and bar 2 respectively. In earlier exercises we experienced "finding our way about" within the triad (Chapter IX). Here are some similar Exercises using the V^7 chord.

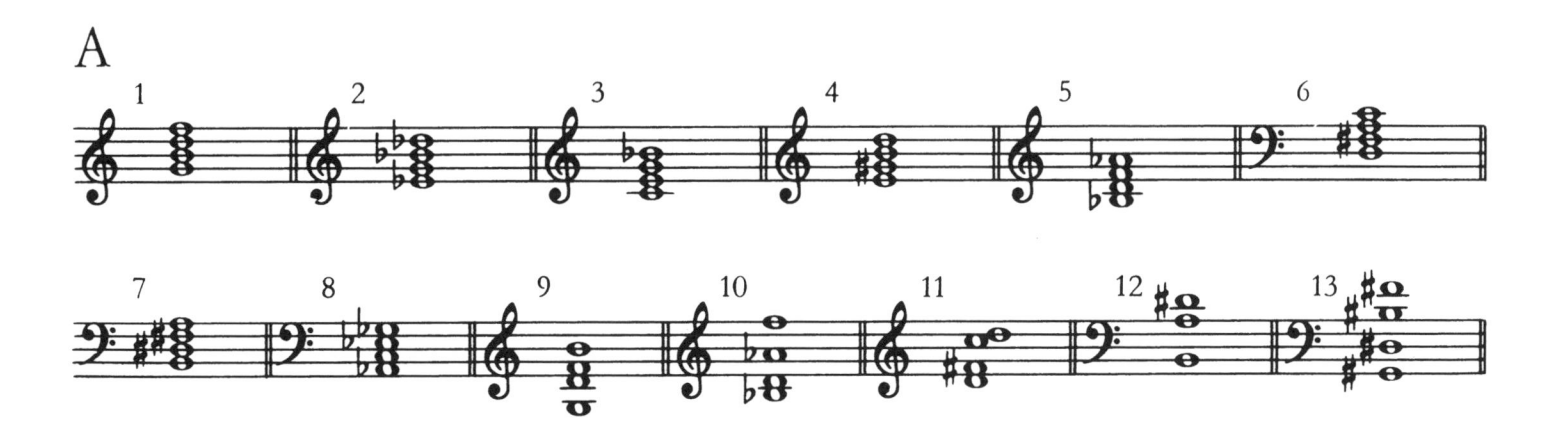

A

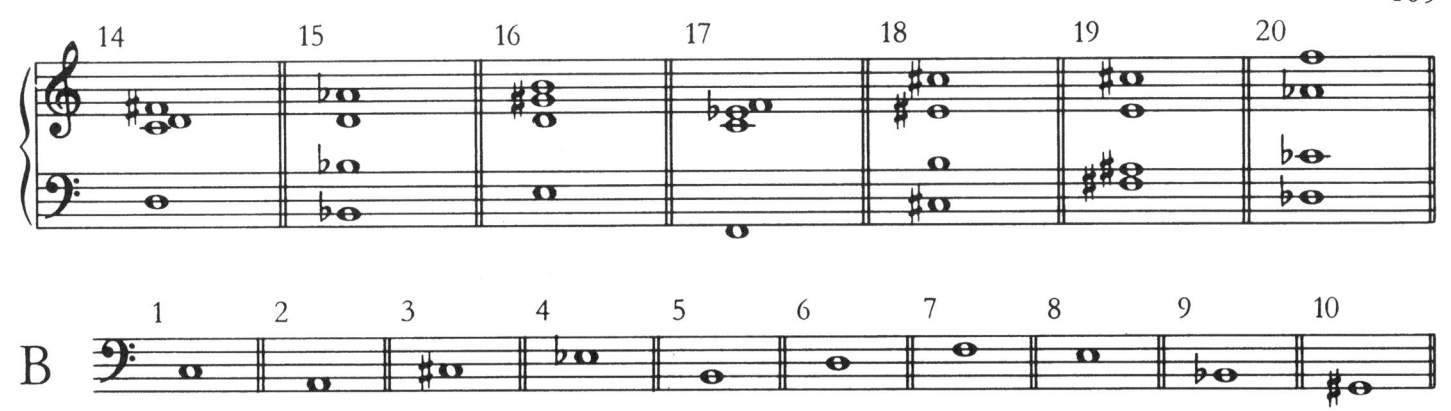

Exercises:

1) Play the above V^7 chords and their resolutions. (Refer to page 35).

2) Play the chords with resolutions, but let each chord sound while you sing it, naming the notes. The chords should be sung from the bottom up, starting with the tonic. The chords notated in open position are to be sung as if they were in close position. Chord No.12 therefore is sung:

Note:
In this chapter all the resolutions of the V^7 chords have been notated with the major tonic. However you should practice resolutions to the minor tonic in the same ways.

3) Play the bass note (root) of each chord. Sing the chord. Sing the chords and their resolutions, naming the notes, beginning with the note you have played.

4) From the bass notes notated in Section B, sing the notes of the V^7 chords and their resolutions after first playing them on the piano.

5) Think of the notes below as sevenths in various V^7 chords. Play them on the piano and sing the V^7 chords from the note downwards. Name the notes. Finish with the tonic in the key of resolution.

Using the V⁷ chord, here are some special exercises for the following intervals:

    I. Minor seventh
    II. Augmented fourth (tritone)
    III. Major sixth (It has already been introduced in conjunction with the triad, but here it has a different harmonic function).

I. Minor seventh

1) Sing the minor seventh from the root of the V⁷ chord upwards to the seventh, naming the notes,
(a) from the chords notated in A, page 104, after first playing only the tonic on the piano.
(b) from the bass notes notated in B, page 105.
Sing the minor seventh from the seventh of the V⁷ chord downwards to the root
(a) from the sevenths of the above chords after first playing only the seventh on the piano. If you find it difficult to sing the minor seventh downwards immediately, first think of the descending V⁷ chord as a whole.

(b) from the treble notes in Exercise 5, page 105.

II. Augmented fourth (tritone)

This interval is formed by the movement from the seventh of the V⁷ chord upwards to the third of the chord. In terms of the step numbers of the key of resolution, this is the interval between the fourth and seventh degrees, 4/7. This resolution yields two notes previously studied. Thus the normal major/minor tonal resolution of the dissonant augmented fourth is:

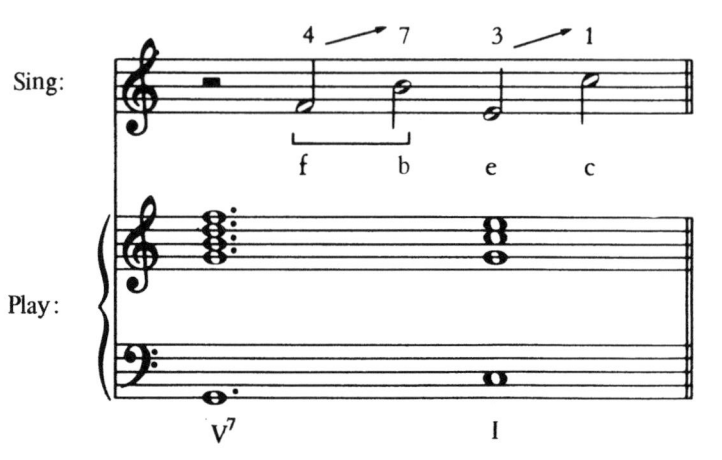

Exercise:

1) Let us study again the V^7 chords on page 104. Each chord contains an augmented fourth. Play the chords and their resolutions, and at the same time sing the augmented fourth and its resolution according to the formula 4/7, 3/1. See the example at the bottom of page 106.

2) Play only the root of each V^7 chord with the left hand in the bass. While this note is sounding, sing first the minor seventh (without help from the piano) and then go upwards to the third in the V^7 chord. Then play the root of the chord in the bass while you sing the resolution of the tritone to a minor sixth. Here is the exercise notated:

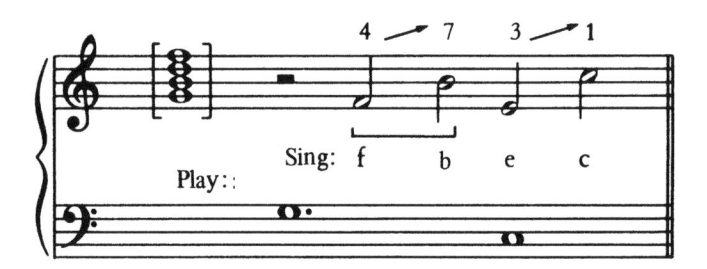

(3) Do the same as in Exercise (2), except in downward motion, as follows:

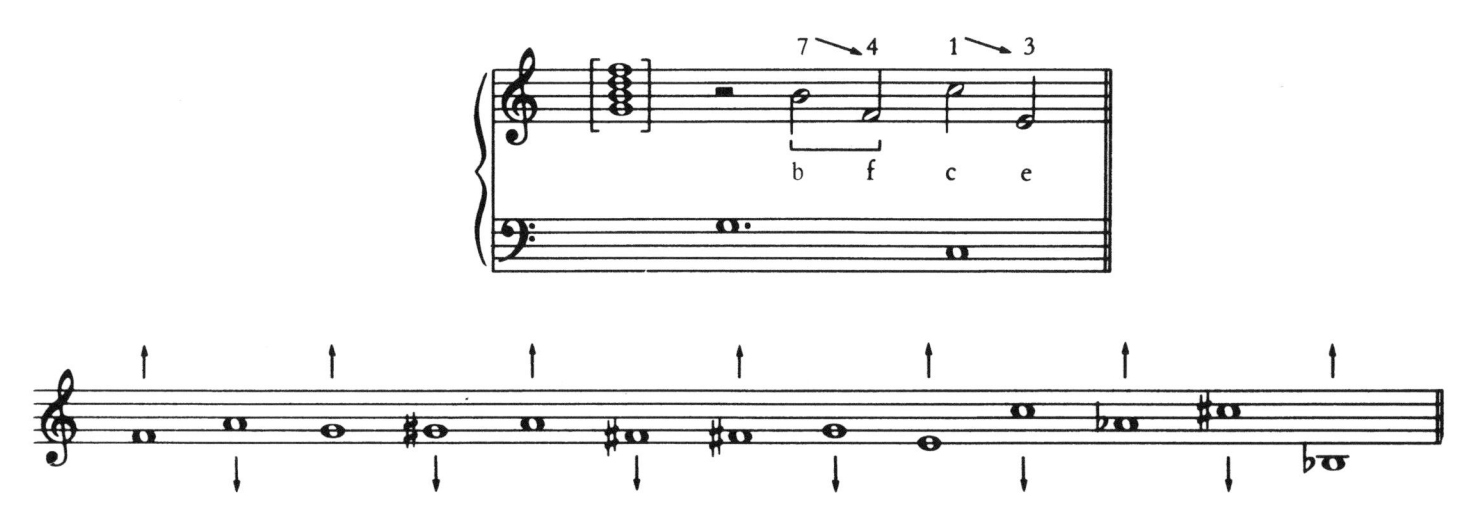

(4) Begin on the above notes and sing the augmented fourth with subsequent resolution to the minor sixth. Always name the notes. The arrows indicate the direction of the movement.

III. Major sixth from the V⁷ chord

The major sixth shown here has the following position in the V⁷ chord:

from the fifth of the V⁷ down to the seventh of the chord.

Exercise:

1) Play the V⁷ chords on page 104. Sing each chord the way as shown above and name the notes.
2) Do the same, treating each note in Exercise 5, page 105, as the fifth of a V⁷ chord. Play only the first note and sing the others without help from the piano. If the exercise is too difficult at first, you might find it helpful to play the root of the V⁷ chord in the bass, that is, the fifth below the first note. Look at the following example:

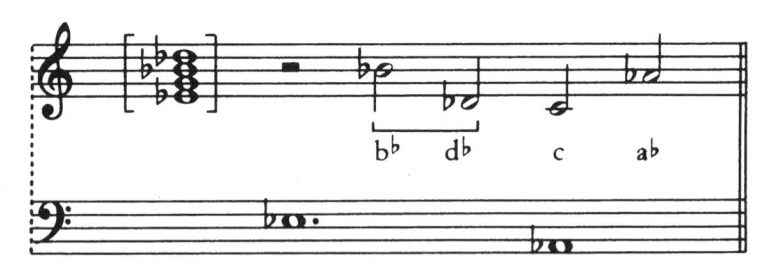

b♭   d♭   c   a♭

Play only if necessary (see No. 2 above).

3) These notes are to be used as sevenths of the V⁷ chord. Sing 7→5 of the V⁷ chord with its appropriate resolution, using the following as a model:

The inversions of the V⁷ chord

It is assumed that the inversions of the V⁷ chord are familiar to you from your harmony studies. For your information however, the V⁷ chord is presented below with its inversions and resolutions, along with some suggestions for practice.

V⁷ in root position. The root and bass notes of the chord are identical: g. Figured bass: 7, "chord of the seventh".

V⁷ with the third in the bass (first inversion). Root: g. Bass note: b (the third). Figures bass: $^6_5$, more often $^6_5{}_3$, a "six-five" chord because of the presence of a sixth and a fifth above the bass.

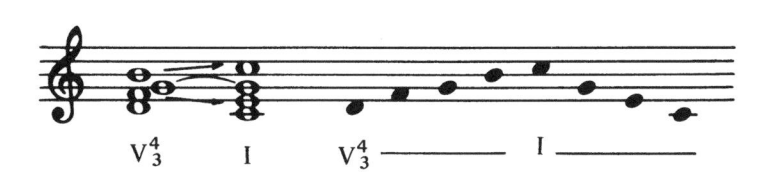

V⁷ with the fifth in the bass (second inversion). Root: g. Bass note: d (the lowest fifth of the chord). Figured bass $^6_4$ more often $^4_3$, a "four-three" chord because of the presence of a third and a fourth above the bass.

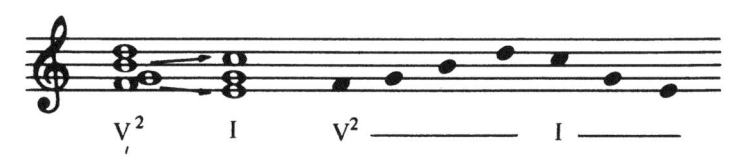

V⁷ with the seventh in the bass (third inversion). Root: g. Bass note: f (the seventh of the chord). Figured bass: $^6_4{}_2$ often $^4_2$ or just 2, a "four-two" chord because af the presence of a second and a fourth above the bass.

V⁷ with the root omitted, the so-called imperfect dominant:

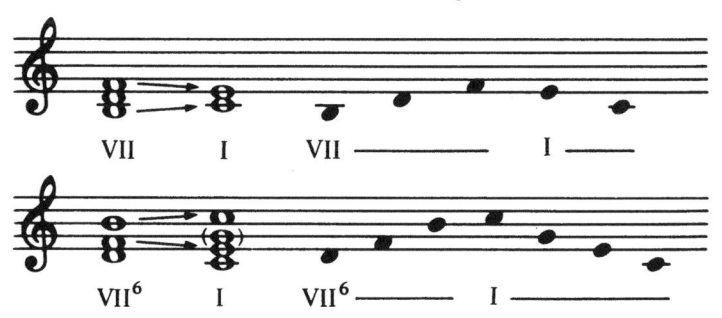

See page 35.

Often written V⁰ (Figured bass: $^6_3$).

Exercise:

1) Sing and name the notes of the V_5^6, V_3^4, and V_2^4 chords from the bass notes in Example B, page 105. Use the method outlined on the previous page that uses the small black notes after each chord.

2) A difficult but effective exercise is to sing and name the notes of a whole series of chords, always beginning from the same bass note. The following series is recommended.

   (a) major triad
   (b) minor triad
   (c) sixth chord in minor
   (d) sixth chord in major
   (e) six-four chord in major
   (f) six-four chord in minor
   (g) diminished triad with resolution
   (h) V^7 with resolution
   (i) V_5^6 with resolution
   (j) V_3^4 with resolution
   (k) V_2^4 with resolution

From the note C:

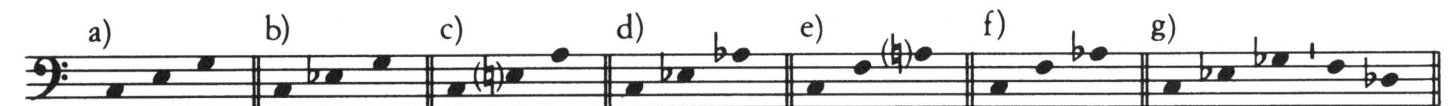

Melodies:

Andante larghetto

2. But thou didst not leave his soul in hell;
But thou didst not leave his soul in hell;

3. Ach, Brü-der, ach, Brü-der, ihr geht ja mir vor-ü-ber, als wär's mit mir vor-bei, als wär's mit mir vor-bei!

Andante

4. Con-fu-ta-tis ma-le-dic-tis flam-mis a-cri-bus ad-dic-tis ma-le-dic-tis, flam-mis a-cri-bus ad-dic-tis

Menuett

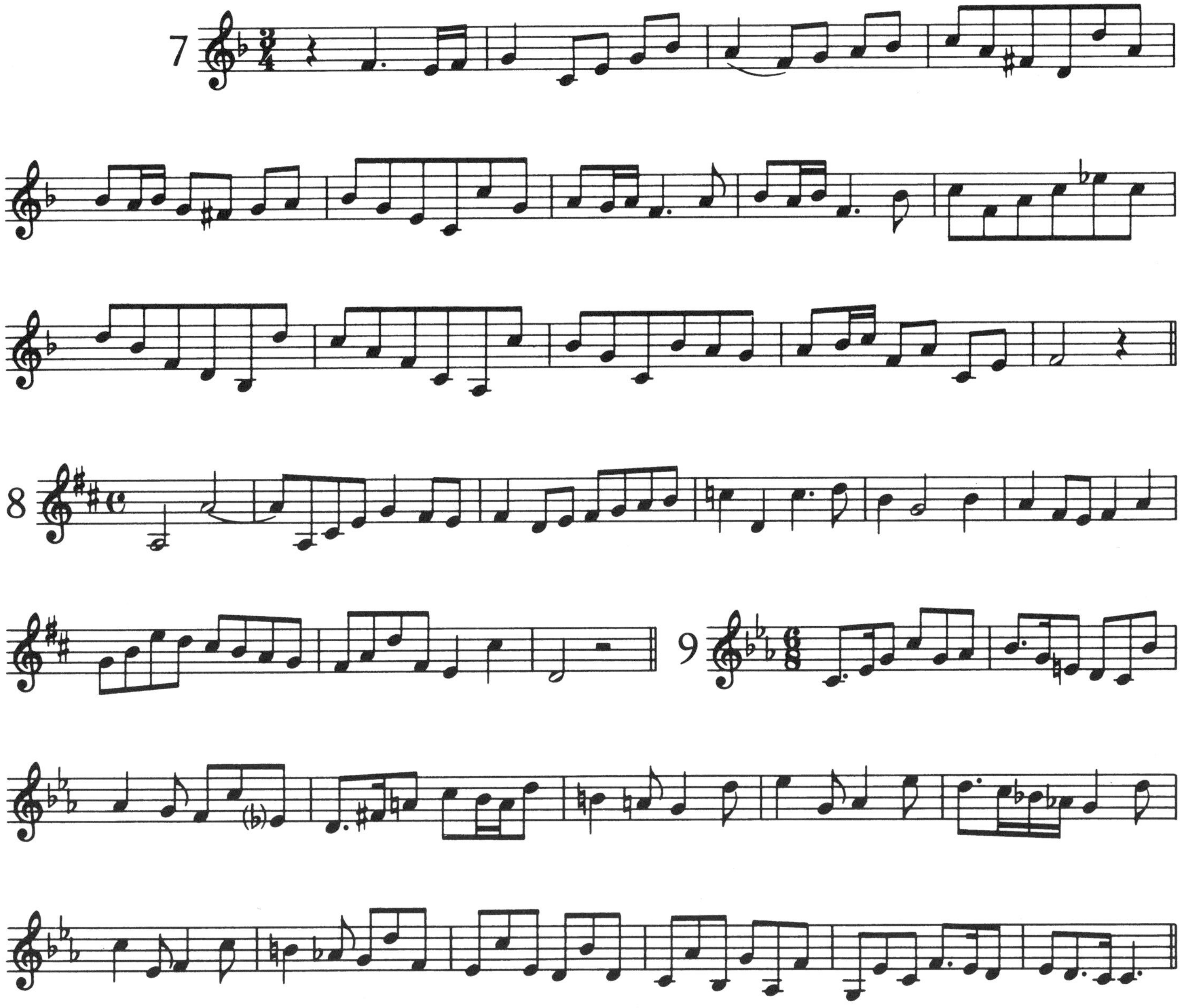
7
8
9

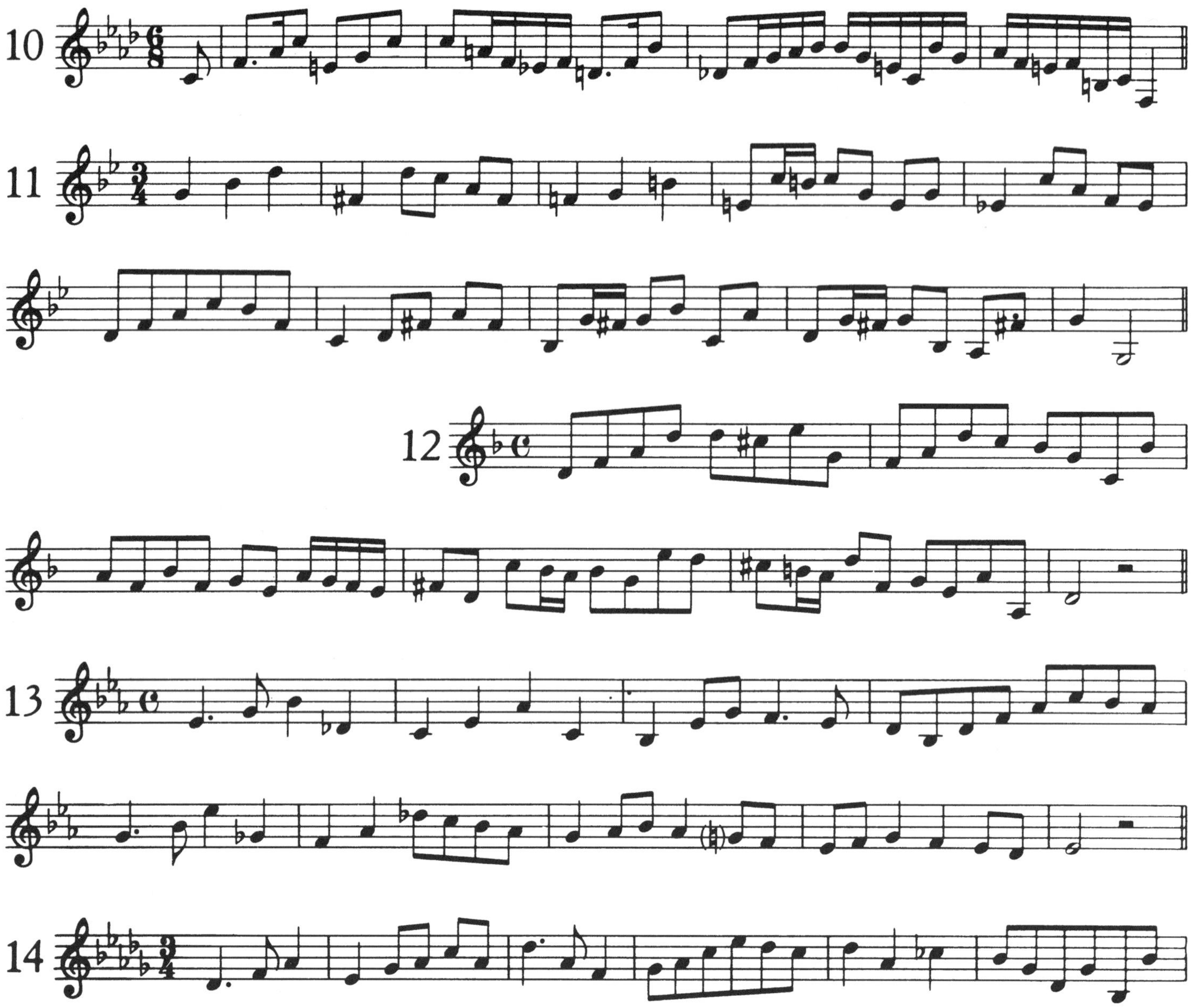
10
11
12
13
14

Examples Nos. 1 - 14 are well suited to harmonic exercises according to the suggestions on page 6.

15. Nun Herr, was soll ich mich trö - sten, mich trö - -sten?

16. **Allegro larghetto**

17. **Largo**

20. Öf - ver vå - gors klara spegelar Du mig bort, mig hem - åt för; Vid din sida säll jag seglar. Resans längd min fröjd ej stör.

21. Evangelist: Denn solches ist geschehen, auf daß die Schrift erfüllet würde! **Adagio** Ihr sollet ihm kein Bein zerbrechen.

22. Evangelist: Da ging Pilatus zu ihnen hinaus und sprach: Pilatus: Was bringet ihr für Klage wider diesen Menschen? Evangelist: Sie antworteten und sprachen zu ihm:

Jesus:

23. Ich habe frei, öffentlich geredet vor der Welt. Ich habe allezeit gelehret in der Schule, und in dem Tempel, da alle Juden zusammenkommen, und habe nichts im Verborg'nen geredt. Was fragest du mich darum? Frage die darum, die gehöret haben, was ich zu

ih - nen ge - re - det ha - be; sie - he, die - sel - bi - gen wis - sen, was ich ge - sa - get ha - be!

24. Evangelist: Und da sie ihn ver - spot - tet hat - ten, zo - gen sie ihm den Man - tel aus und zo - gen ihm sei - ne Klei - der an und füh - re - ten ihn hin, daß sie ihn kreu - - - zigten.

25. Jesus: Stecke dein Schwert an seinen Ort; denn wer das Schwert nimmt, der soll durchs Schwert umkommen. Oder meinest du, daß ich nicht könnte meinen Vater bitten, daß er mir zuschickte mehr denn zwölf Legion Engel? Wie würde aber die Schrift erfüllet? Es muß also gehen.

XVI. The dominant ninth chord (V⁹)
The dominant ninth chord with a lowered ninth and the root omitted (a diminished seventh chord) Secondary seventh chords. Diminished third in conjunction with the Neapolitan sixth chord.

The dominant ninth chord

We have worked with triads and sevenths and we have seen the great importance of the interval of the third in major/minor harmony and melody. In fact in major/minor tonal harmony the third is the basis of the chords.

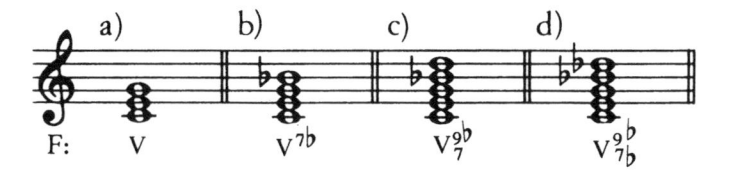

We recognize the chords (a) and (b) from earlier studies. (c) is a chord of the ninth, a chord of the dominant ninth, V^9, in f major. The V^9 consists of the V^7 chord plus the addition of a major third above the seventh. This new note forms a major ninth from the tonic. Hence the name the chord of the ninth. In its normal resolution, this ninth can move either up or down:

The ninth also can be minor (see (d) above). In minor it assumes the function of a leading tone to the root of the chord and the normal resolution is downwards to this note:

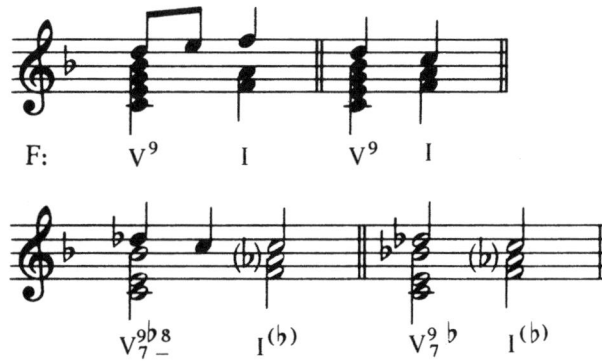

Exercise: Practice the resolutions of V^9 in major and minor on the piano.

Both the major and minor V⁹ were used extensively during the Romantic period. Late nineteenth-century music contains many examples of both melody and harmony influenced by the chord of the ninth. Here are two familiar examples:

César Franck: Sonata A-maj. for violin and piano

Richard Wagner: Tristan and Isolde, Act. II

Some composers went even further in piling up thirds. Study the following example from Richard Wagner's Prelude to the third act of *Lohengrin*:

The melody is based clearly on a chord built of thirds, and it adds another third to the chord of the ninth!

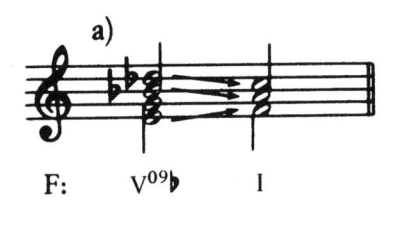

In the above example the sign V⁰⁹♭ stands for a V⁰ chord in first inversion with the root omitted. The bass note is thus the third of the V⁰ chord. From this third (e) up to the ninth of the V⁰ (d♭) a diminished seventh is formed, which explains the figured bass notation "diminished seventh chord", e g e♭ d♭. This chord, which consists of three minor thirds, contains strong leading tone tendencies (see the arrows in example a) and therefore has a very marked tendency to resolve to the triad which follows.

Exercises:

1) Play again the seventh chords in B, Chapter XVI, page 105. While the chords are sounding, sing the appropriate dimished seventh, beginning with the third of the V⁷ chord. Also sing their resolutions. No. 1 in B, page 105, will be performed in this manner:

Sing: e g b♭ d♭   c a(♭) f

Play:

2) Sing, naming the notes, the diminished sevenths with their resolutions (also to minor triads) as in the musical example b) above, using the following notes as starting tones:

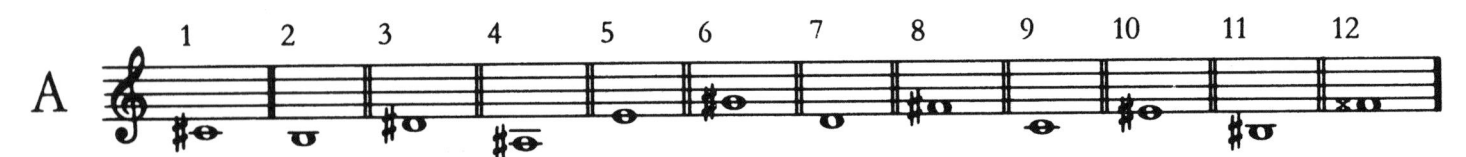

A

(3) The notes below are to be regarded as diminished sevenths (lowered ninth in a V^9 chord). Sing, naming the notes, diminished sevenths *downwards*, as well as their resolutions according to the method outlined below.

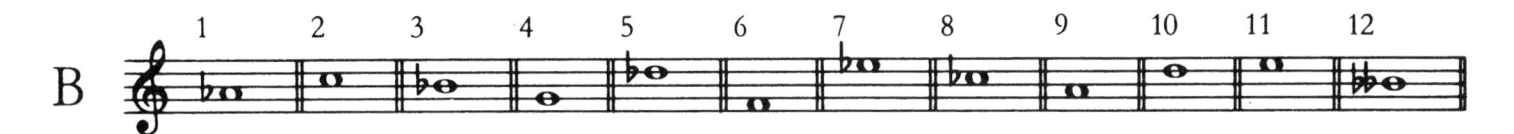

B

(Name the notes!)

4) Use the notes in A and sing diminished sevenths with their resolutions in the following way:

(Name the notes!)

(5) Use the notes in B and sing diminished sevenths with their resolutions in the following way:

(Name the notes!)

In some cases it may be difficult to see the tonality in an arpeggiated diminished seventh chord
(a) if the notes extend beyond the basic chord (if the third of the V^9 is the lowest note).
(b) if there are big leaps within the notes of the chord. Examples:

The tonal stability of a chord is derived from a clear feeling of the tonic, and knowing where the tonic is, the relationship of the notes becomes apparent. But in the diminished seventh chord this tonic is omitted and can be hard to determine, even visually. The tonic of the chord can be located as follows: when the chord if arpeggiated, as in a), there always occurs an augmented second (here d♭ e♮). The top note in this interval is the third of the $V^{o9♭}$ chord in question. Its tonic therefore lies a major third below (in this case c). The same reasoning applies to example b), even if the augmented second is somewhat harder to find here because of the chord's open position. To stabilize your intonation when practicing melodies like a) and b) (and exercises 4 and 5 on page 125), you are allowed to play the omitted tonic on the piano.

Secondary seventh chords

All intervals are not obtained from the V^7 chord. A non-dominant seventh chord has these characteristics:

a) it lacks a diminished fifth, with its strong tendency to resolve.
b) the seventh can be major.
c) its third may be minor.

These so-called secondary seventh chords can be formed on all degrees of the scale except the fifth and seventh, whose sevenths are always dominant, V^7 and V^9_3 respectively.

I IV^7 V^{o9} III^7 VI II^7 V^7 I

Secondary seventh chords and melodies characterized by their sevenths are usually sequential and the tonics of the cords fall in a series of fifths. Study the following excerpt from J.S. Bach's Invention in D minor:

Study only the melodies and then compare them with the outlined harmonic progression. Even if the secondary sevenths are not prominent in the Bach excerpt, the basis of this example is the same type of harmonic progression as found in the previous C major example.

Once your ear has absorbed the harmonic progression, it is not usually difficult to sing sevenths in this kind of melodic context.

Another way of comprehending the sevenths in the melody is to hear them with the missing thirds in the key.

The diminished third

The diminished third often occurs in a melody in conjunction with the Neapolitan sixth chord ($II^{6\flat}$). Its definite leading tone tendency towards the tonic makes it easy to sing.

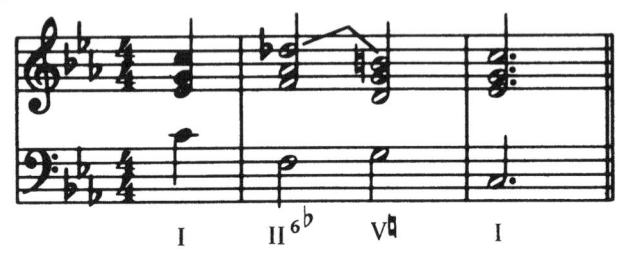

I $II^{6\flat}$ V♮   I

Exercise: Sing the melody in the above example in a number of keys. Name the notes! Play only the bass notes on the piano.

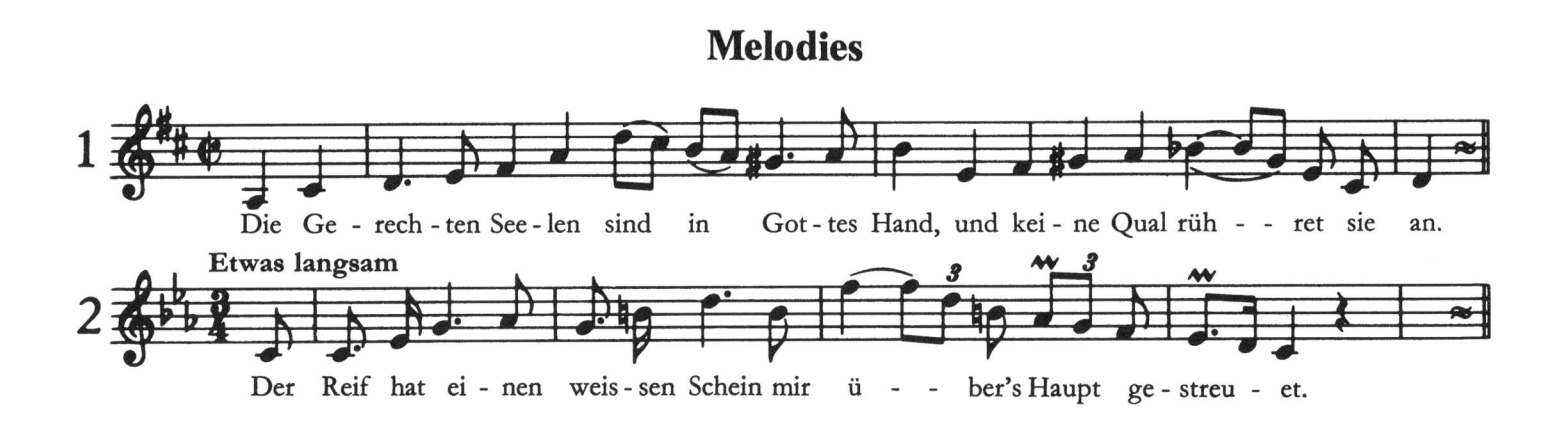

Melodies

1. Die Ge - rech - ten See - len sind in Got - tes Hand, und kei - ne Qual rüh - - ret sie an.

Etwas langsam

2. Der Reif hat ei - nen weis - sen Schein mir ü - - ber's Haupt ge - streu - et.

Larghetto

3. How beau-ti-ful are the feet of them that preach the gos-pel of peace.

Allegro

4. Ky - rie - e   e - le - - i - son

5. And with his stripes are we hea - - led.

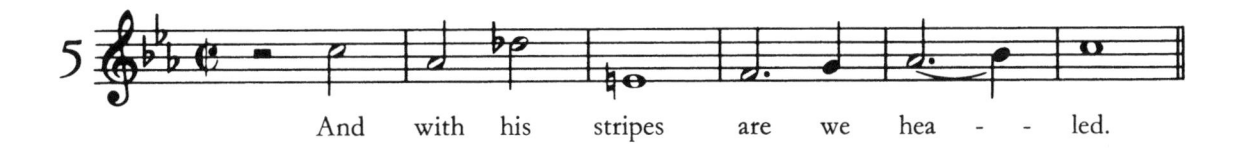

6.

Andante larghetto

7. For be-hold! Darkness shall co-ver the earth and gross darkness the people, and gross darkness the people.

130

Courante

8

Prélude

9

10

Zer - flie - ße, mein Her - ze, in Flu - ten der Zäh - ren

13. Af de mörka tankar e-vigt plå-gas jag, e-vigt plå-gas jag.

14. Jesus: Wahrlich, ich sa-ge dir: In die-ser Nacht, e-he der Hahn krä-het, wirst du mich dreimal ver-leug-nen.

Jesus: Was bekümmert ihr das Weib? Sie hat ein gut Werk an mir getan! Ihr habet allezeit Arme bei euch, mich aber habt ihr nicht allezeit. Daß sie dies Wasser hat auf meinen Leib gegossen, hat sie getan, daß man mich begraben wird.

Evangelist: Darnach bat Pilatum Joseph von Arimathia, der ein

Jünger Jesu war, (doch heimlich aus Furcht vor den Juden,) daß er möchte abnehmen den Leichnam Jesu. Und Pilatus erlaubete es.

17. Erbarm es Gott! Hier steht der Heiland angebunden. O Geißelung, o Schläg', o Wunden! Ihr Henker, haltet

ein! Er-wei-chet euch der See-len Schmerz, der Anblick sol-ches Jammers nicht? Ach ja, ihr habt ein Herz, das muß der Mar-ter-säu-le gleich und noch viel här-ter sein. Er-barmt euch, hal-tet ein!

Ach Gol-ga-tha, un-sel'-ges Gol-ga-tha! Der Herr der Herrlichkeit muß schimpflich hier ver-der-ben, der Se-gen und das Heil der Welt wird als ein Fluch an's Kreuz ge-stellt. Dem Schöpfer Himmels und der Er-den soll Erd' und Luft ent-zo-gen werden; die Unschuld muß hier schuldig ster-ben. Das ge-het meiner See-le nah; ach Gol-ga-tha, un-sel'-ges Gol-ga-tha!

19

Drick ur ditt glas, se döden på dig vän-tar, sli-par sitt svärd och vid din tröskel står.
Bliv ej förskräckt, han blott på gravdörrn glän-tar, slår den i-gen kans-ke än på ett år. Movitz, din lungsot den drar dig i graven. [Violoncell] Knäpp nu ok-ta-ven; stäm di-na strängar, sjung om li-vets vår! Stäm di-na strängar sjung om li-vets vår. [Violoncell]

20 Poco Allegretto

Så dys-ter ungmön satt en qväll på haf-vets strand; den vän hon haft så kär gått bort till fjer-ran land. Då steg en fée ur vå-gen upp, ur vå-gen upp och bad med kär - - - lig röst: Kom med, kom med! och ung - - - - mön sjönk till hen-nes kal-la bröst.

21 men Gudmund er en tro-fast svend.

22 I kveld skal in-gen her på går-den vi-de, att Gudmund er fredløs; i mor-gen får han se at hjael-pe sig selv

23 Den vok-ser som e-gen i å-re-ne lan-ge; den naeres ved tankar och sorger og –

24 Ha-vet su-sar, sko-gen skälver, ju-ni-nat-ten trå-nar blek. Sil--ver-vatt-rad dy-ning väl-ver, halvt i dröm och halvt i lek, en en-sam stjärnas spegling.

25 Con brio, e rubato
Och vill du väl, så får du väl, så har du väl min he-la själ till träl att älska och pina och trampa i-hjäl med tramp av din häl, du hö-ga du svin-ga-de vil-da i dansen.

Mäßig langsam

26

As we have noticed several times earlier, confidence in melody reading comes not from singing individual intervals, but from a thorough understanding of combinations of intervals. These combinations are given here in tonal form, often combined with harmonic progressions. The movements of one chord to another create the harmonic progressions of a composition. Security in melody reading also implies the ability to read quickly and to understand the harmonic progressions.

In the following example from Wagner, the sight reading demands are great because the composer has exploited the chromatic potential of the tonal system to the full. It also is difficult to find and analyze the tonal center. It is quite worthwhile to become thoroughly familiar with this type of material. Here again the sight reading procedure is based upon knowledge of music theory.

In teaching groups of three to five students, the author has used the following method in studying the Wagner example and similar material:

1) The student first should attempt to discover the harmonic progressions in either the complete example or in a small portion of it (possibly with the guidance of the teacher).

2) The teacher (and later the student) should play the harmonic progressions by reducing the accompaniment to the basic chordal patterns (so-called harmonic reduction).

A reduction of Example No. 27 on page 140 could take the following form:

3) One student (or several students) should sing the solo part (first without text) while the teacher or another student plays the harmonic reduction.

4) One student should sing the solo part to a piano part which is reduced even further, one which possibly contains only the bass notes or roots of each chord.

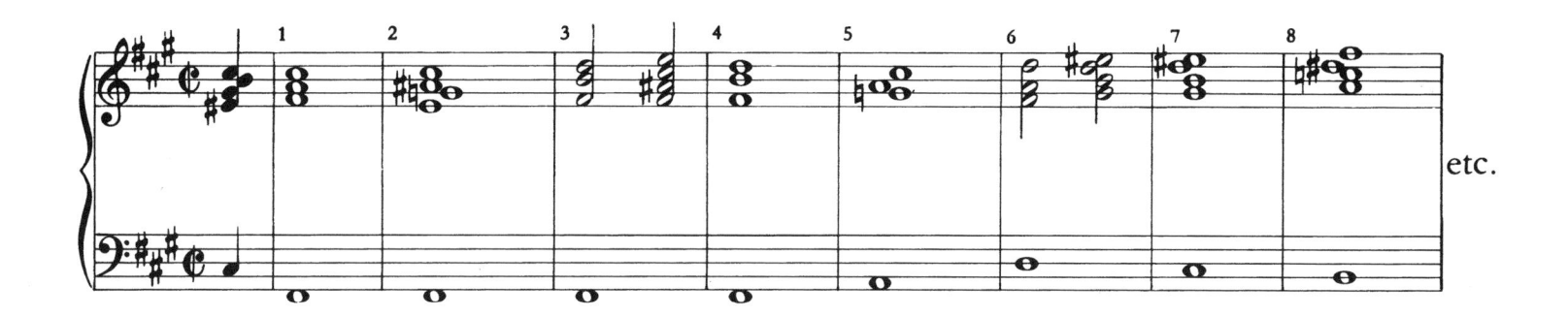

(1) The author is aware of the frequent use of the term "leading-tone triad" and the symbol VII^6, but he feels his terminology has stronger meaning in terms of harmonic function.

(2) The cadential $^6_4$ chord here is given the function symbols V$^6_4$ - $^5_3$ (rather than I$^6_4$ – V), because the author feels this shows the tone function more clearly.

The author prefers the term dominant ninth chord with omitted root, just as he preferred the term dominant seventh chord with omitted root.

Sehr lebhaft

Durch dich mußt' ich verlieren mein' Ehr', all meinen Ruhm; nie soll mich Lob mehr zie-ren, Schmach ist mein Hel-den-tum! Die Acht ist mir ge-sprochen, zer-trüm-mert liegt mein Schwert, mein Wap-pen ward zer-brochen, ver-

flucht mein Vater-herd! Wo-
hin ich nun mich wen-de, ge-
flohn, gefehmt bin ich, daß

ihn mein Blick nicht schän - de, flieht selbst der Räu - ber mich. Durch dich, durch dich mußt' ich ver- lie - ren mein' Ehr', all meinen Ruhm; nie soll mich Lob mehr zie - ren, Schmach ____ ist mein Hel - den - tum! Die Acht ist mir ge-

sprochen, zer - trüm - - - mert liegt mein

Schwert, mein Wap - - pen ward zer-brochen, ver - flucht mein Va - ter - herd! O, hätt ich Tod er - ko - ren, da ich so e - lend bin!

Mein' Ehr', mein' Ehr' hab ich ver-lo-ren mein' Ehr', mein' Ehr' ist hin! Mein' Ehr', mein' Ehr' ist hin!

Mäßig langsam

28. Ta - test du's wirklich? Wähnst du das?

Sieh ihn dort, den treu-sten al-ler Treuen; blick auf

ihn, den freundlichsten der Freunde; sei-ner Treu-e frei-ste

Tat traf mein Herz mit feindlichstem Ver-rat!

Trog mich Tristan, sollt' ich hoffen, was sein Trügen mir getroffen, sei durch Melots Rat, redlich mir bewahrt?

29 End - lich! End - lich!

Le - - ben, o Le - - ben!

Sü — — ßes Le — — ben, mei-nem Tri — stan neu ge — ge — ben!

daß ihr Blick ihn nur nicht er-rei-che, den Hel-den oh-ne Glei-che! Oh, er weiß wohl, wa-rum!

Wer des To-des Nacht liebend erschaut, wem sie ihr

tief Geheimnis vertraut, des Tages Lügen, Ruhm und

Ehr', Macht und Gewinn, so schimmernd hehr, wie eitler Staub der Sonnen sind, sie vor dem zer-spon - nen!

In des Ta - ges eit - lem Wäh - - nen

bleibt ihm ein ein-zig Seh - - - nen, das Seh-nen hin zur heil'-gen Nacht, wo ur-e-wig, ein - zig wahr, Lie - - bes - won - ne ihm lacht!

32 Viol.

33 Tristan: Laß den Tag dem To - - de wei - chen!

Isolde:
Tag und Tod mit glei - chen Strei - chen soll - ten uns -
p
p
p
re Lieb' er - rei - chen?
Tristan:
Uns - re Lie - be? Tri -
p
cresc.
pp dolce

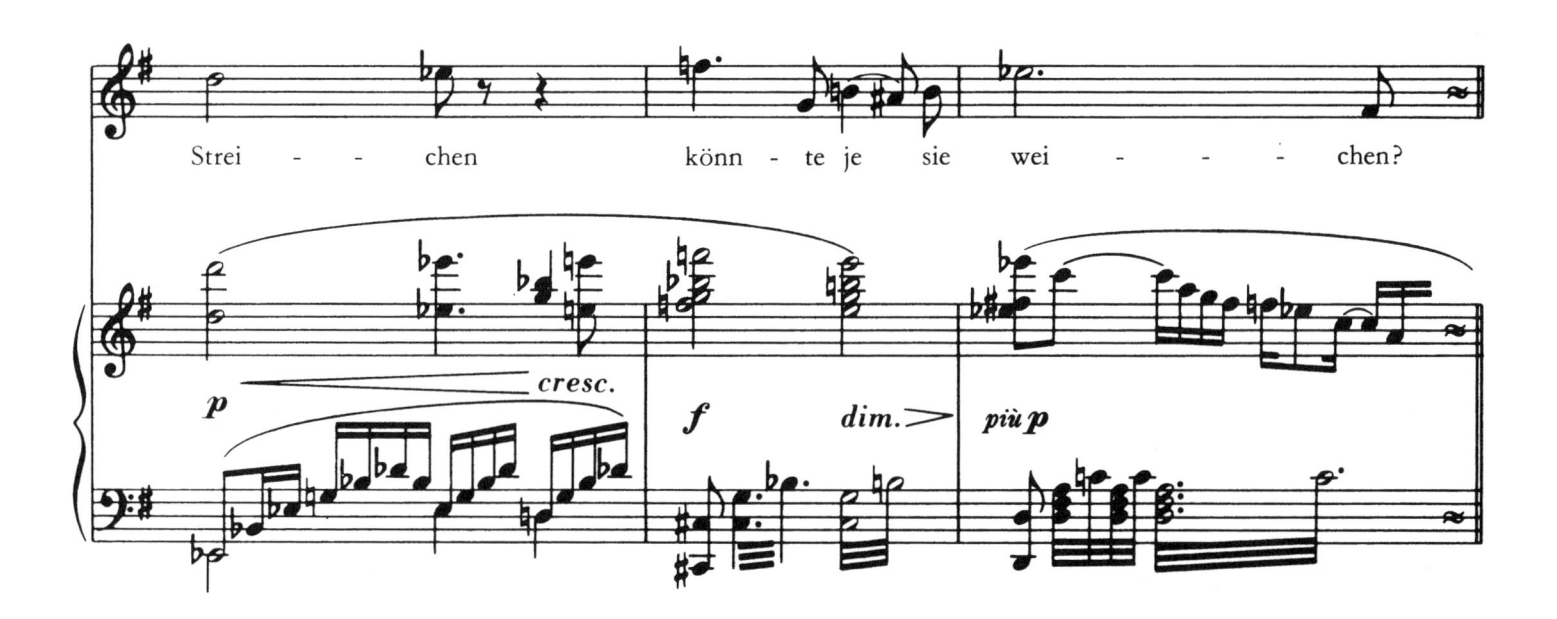

stans Lie - be? Dein' und mein', I-sol - - des Lie - be? Welches To-des

Strei - - chen könn - te je sie wei - - chen?

34. Dünkt dich so wenig, was er dir dankt, bringst du die Irin ihm als Braut, daß er nicht schölte, schlüg ich den Werber, der Urfehde Pfand so treu ihm liefert zur Hand?

35
Isolde:
p
Seh - - nen - der Min - - ne
Tristan:
p
Seh - - nen - der Min - - ne
p
3
schwel - - len - des Blü - - hen, schmach - - ten - der
schwel - - len - des Blü - - hen, schmach - - ten - der
cresc.
3

Lie - be se - li - ges Glüh - en!

Lie - be se - li - ges Glüh - en! Jach

Jach in der Brust jauch - zen-de Lust Tri-

in der Brust jauch - zende Lust! I - sol - de!

stan! Tri - stan! Wel-
I - sol - de! I - sol -
- ten ent - ron - nen, du mir ge-
- de. I - sol -

won - nen, Tri - stan!
de, mir ge - won - nen! I - sol - de!

Du mir ge - won - nen, du mir ein - - - - -
Du mir ein - - zig bewußt,

-zig bewußt, höch - - ste Lie - - -
höch - - - - - ste Lie - -

- - bes - - lust!
- - bes - - lust!

RHYTHM EXERCISES

This section contains ten series of notes (I - X), each with 12 different rhythmic patterns based on them. The 120 examples are arranged mostly by increasing degree of difficulty. They can be used in the following ways:

1. As written dictation

First the student should copy down the series of notes on music paper and then close the book. The teacher will play the examples and the student will notate them. Before the example is played through the first time, the student should be told the meter and the tempo. Then the teacher will play the example, counting out one free measure. Of course this counting must be repeated when necessary before going on to the next example. The number of times the example has to be played will vary according to the degree of difficulty and the student's aptitude. Five attempts may be regarded as average. The time span between them depends on the speed with which the student can write down the notes.

Even students who have no teacher can learn much from this material by using a tape recorder. Each series of examples can be recorded in advance either by the student himself or by someone else. From a practical point of view it is best to record about five versions consecutively, leaving about 10 seconds' pause between each one. This will enable the student to stop the recorder after each playback to do his notating. Information about meter and tempo marking also should be recorded before the first version (the tempo given by counting). Write out all (or half) the examples in any one series before comparing them with the "answers" in the book. It goes without saying that the recording of the examples must be made with great rhythmic precision.

No indications of tempo are given in the examples, although in some cases the rhythmic structure and manner of notation suggest certain interpretations. You should practice taking dictation at different speeds, but for each individual example you should always maintain the same tempo.

Dictation is an effective exercise in comprehension, memory, and notation. It is worth all the time you devote to it!

2. As reading exercises

(a) You can sing the examples as written.
(b) You can read (or sing on one tone) the rhythm only on any syllable.
(c) You can play the examples on an instrument.

3. As material for your own rhythmic invention

Make your own rhythmic patterns for the series of notes. You may find that the degree of difficulty will rise too quickly. Try to remedy this by composing new examples. By comparing the examples in each new series in the book with those in the series immediately preceding it, you will be able to get an idea of how the rhythmic material is expanded. This should suggest ideas for your compositions.

Sections IX and X fall outside the framework of a book such as this one which deals with major/minor tonality, since these sections are based on the twelve-tone series. They have been included for the purpose of introducing the student to tonal material not restricted to a key. The examples serve as an orientation to the practice of music-making in free tonality![1]

(1) See Lars Edlund: **Modus Novus** (Nordiska Musikförlaget)

167

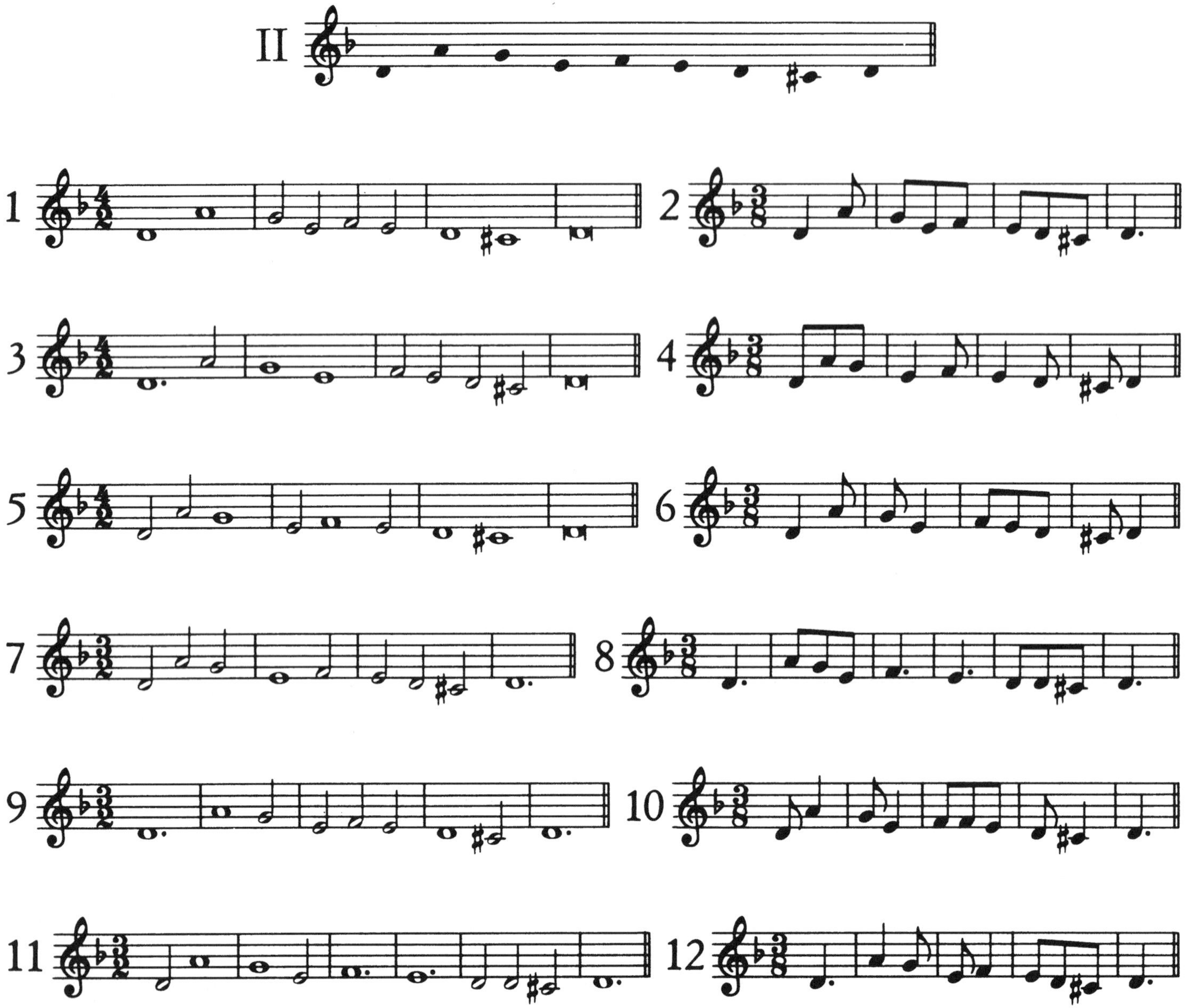
II
1
2
3
4
5
6
7
8
9
10
11
12

169

170

171

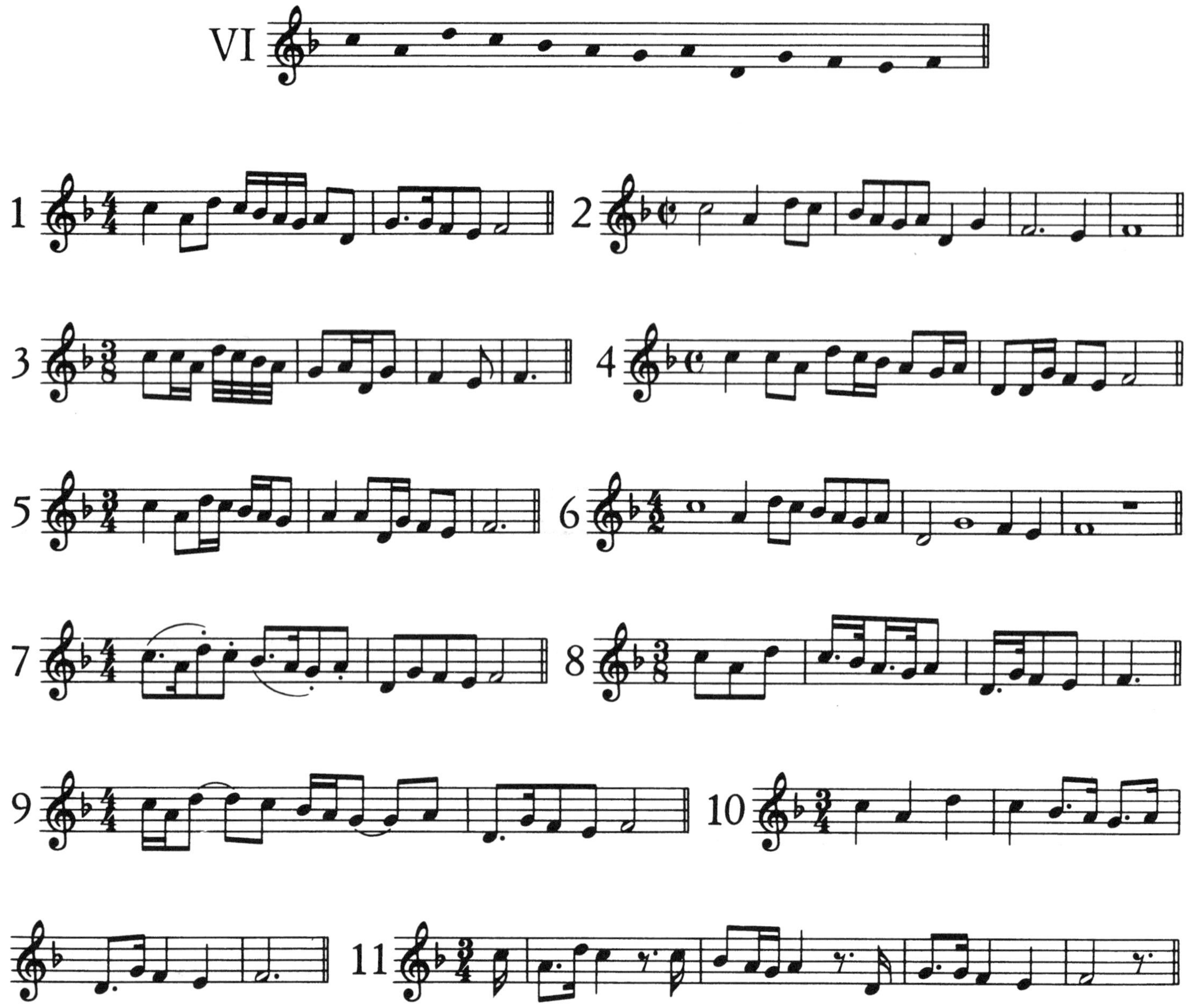
VI
1
2
3
4
5
6
7
8
9
10
11

12 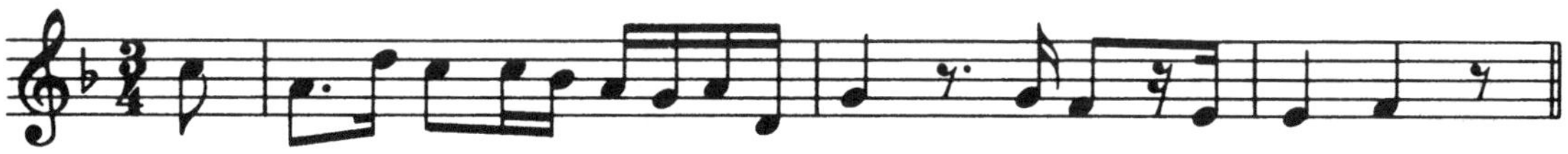

VII 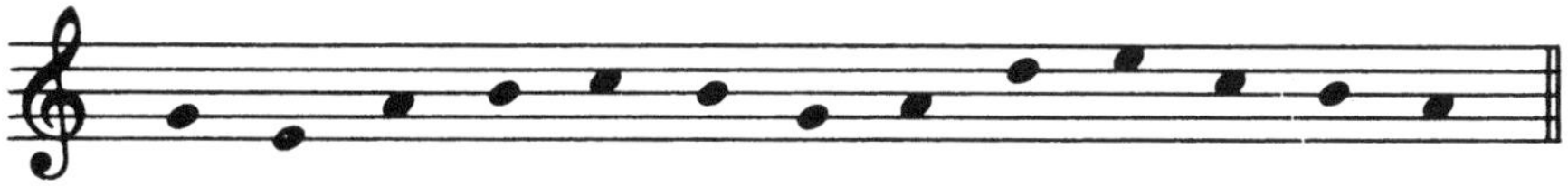

1 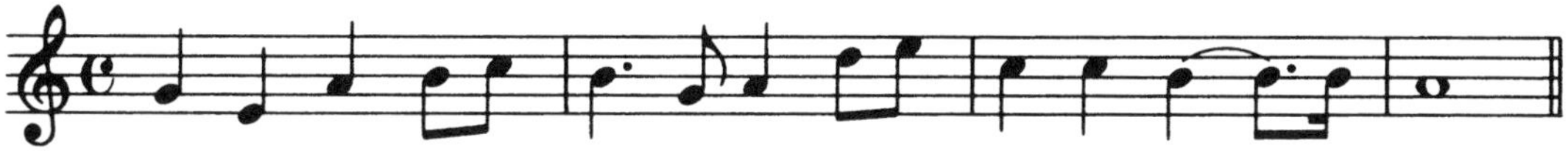

2 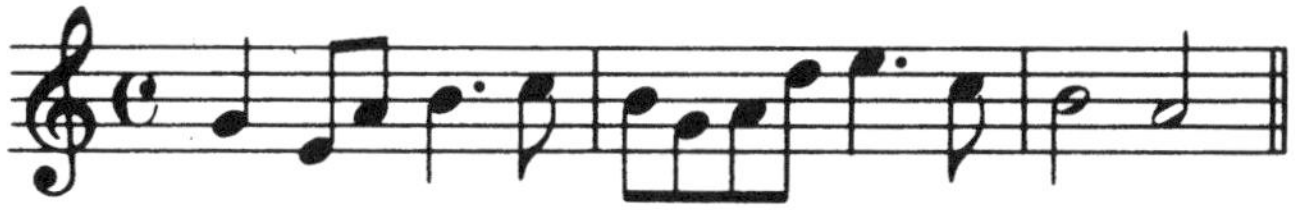

3 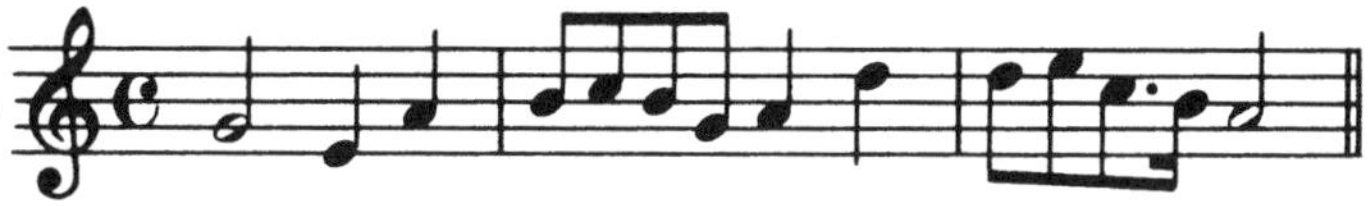

4 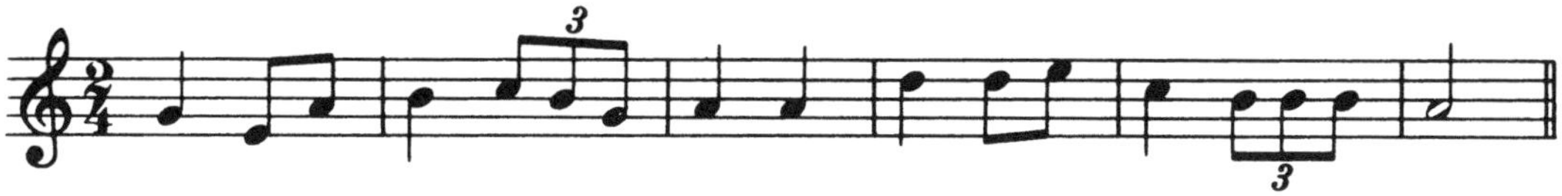

5 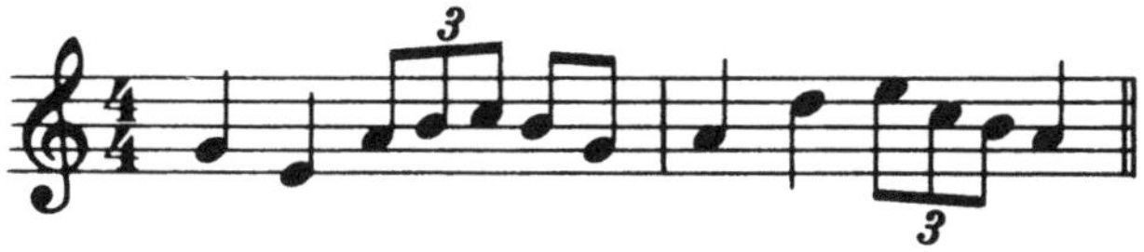

6 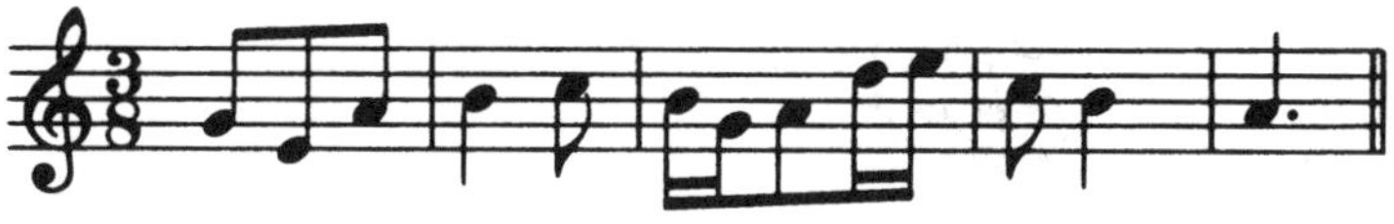

7 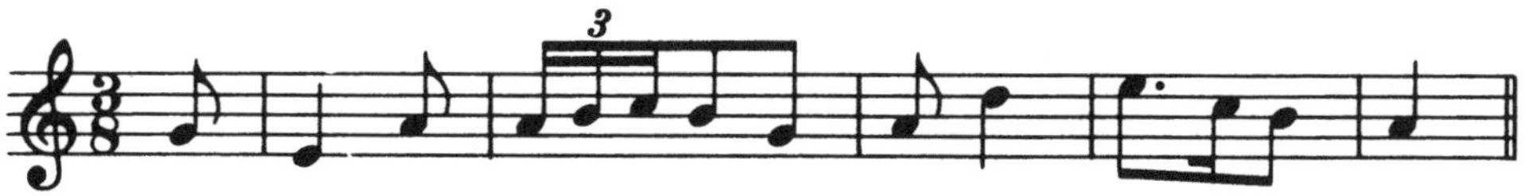

174

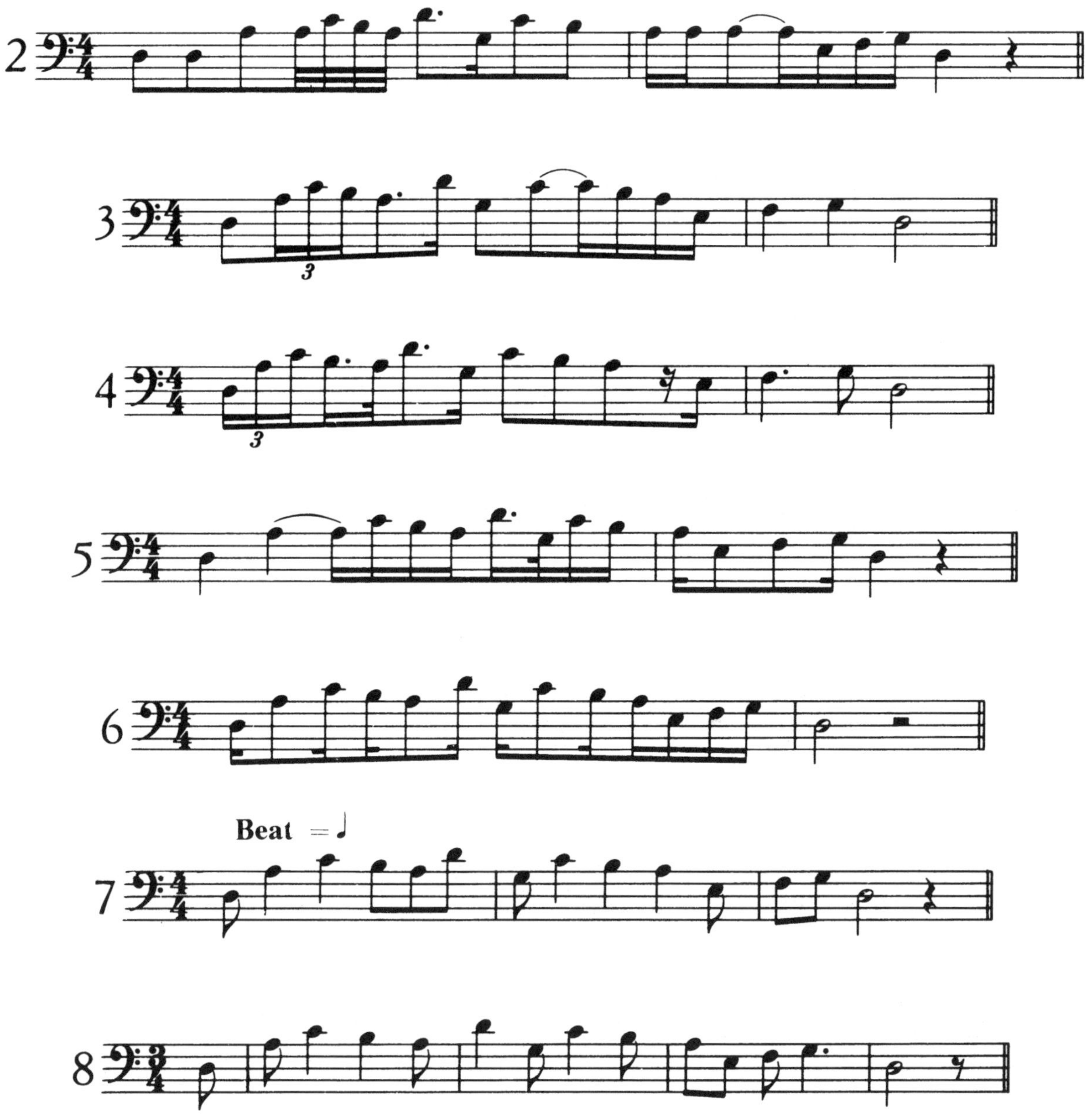
2
3
4
5
6
Beat = ♩
7
8

176

177

11
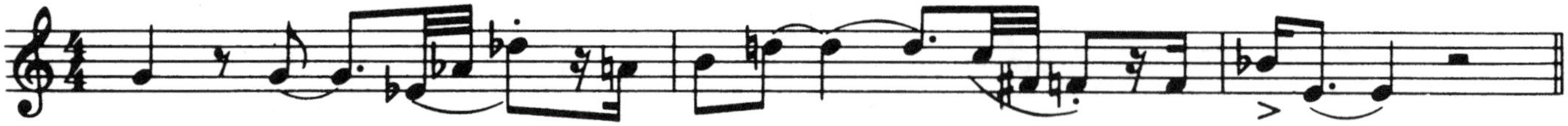

12
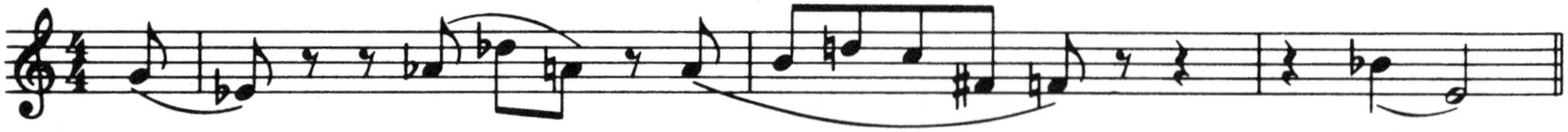

X
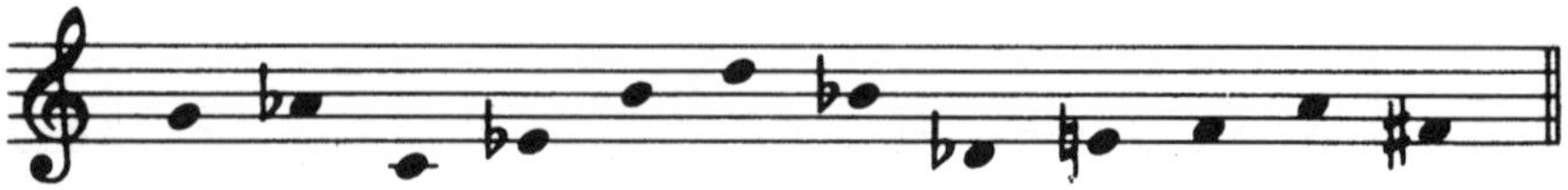

1
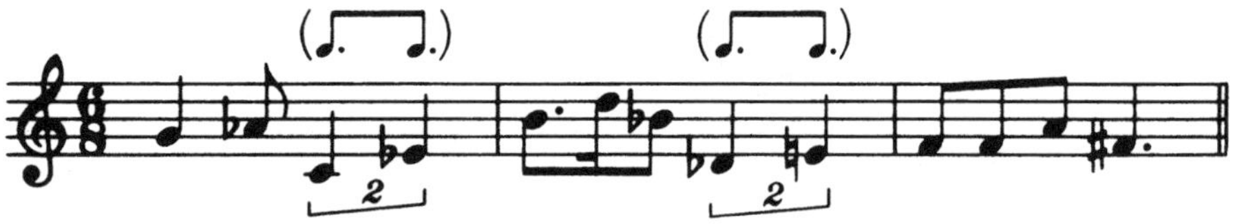

2
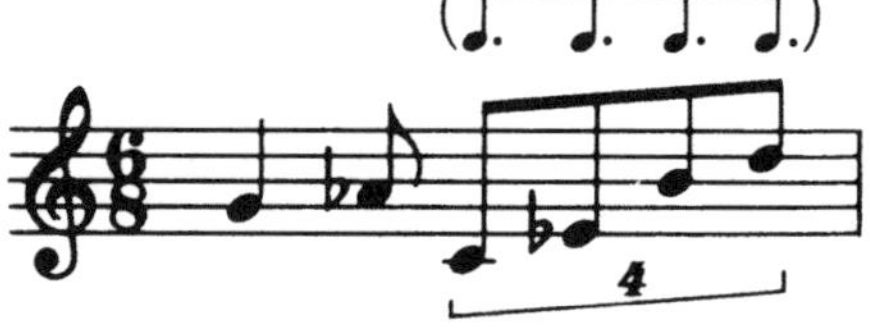

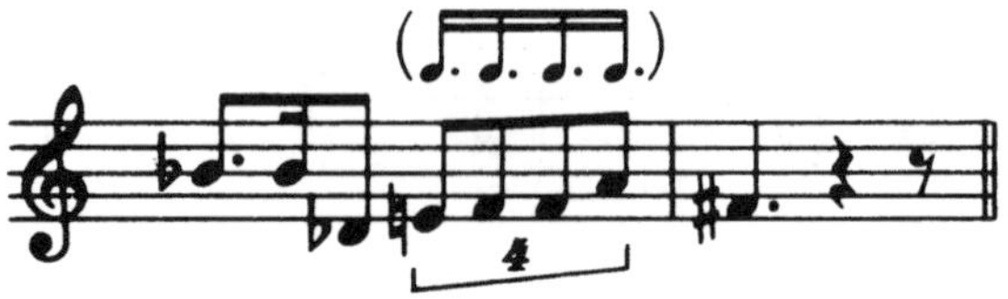

3
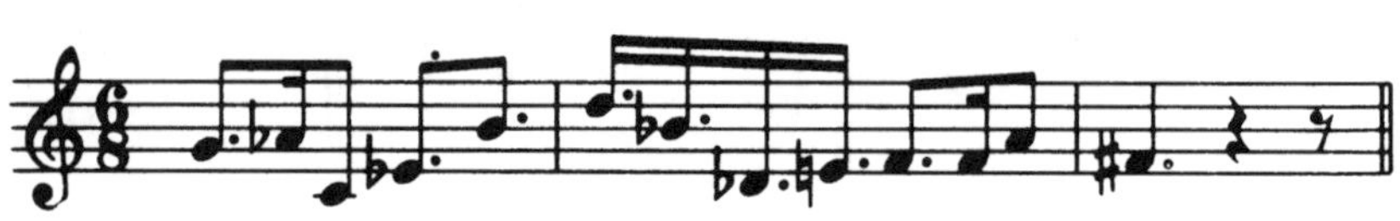

4
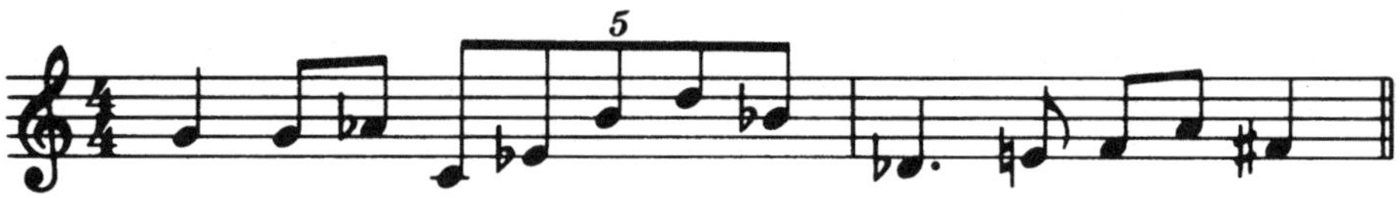

5
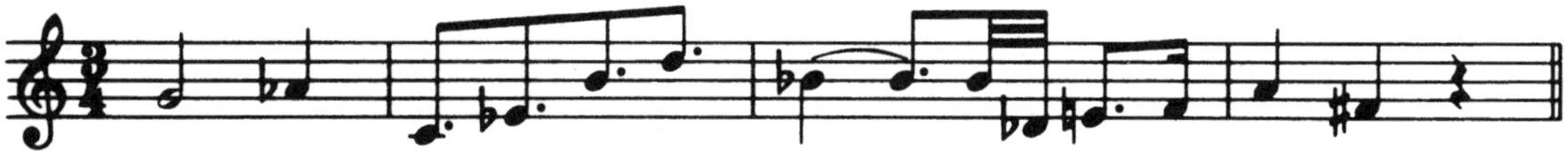

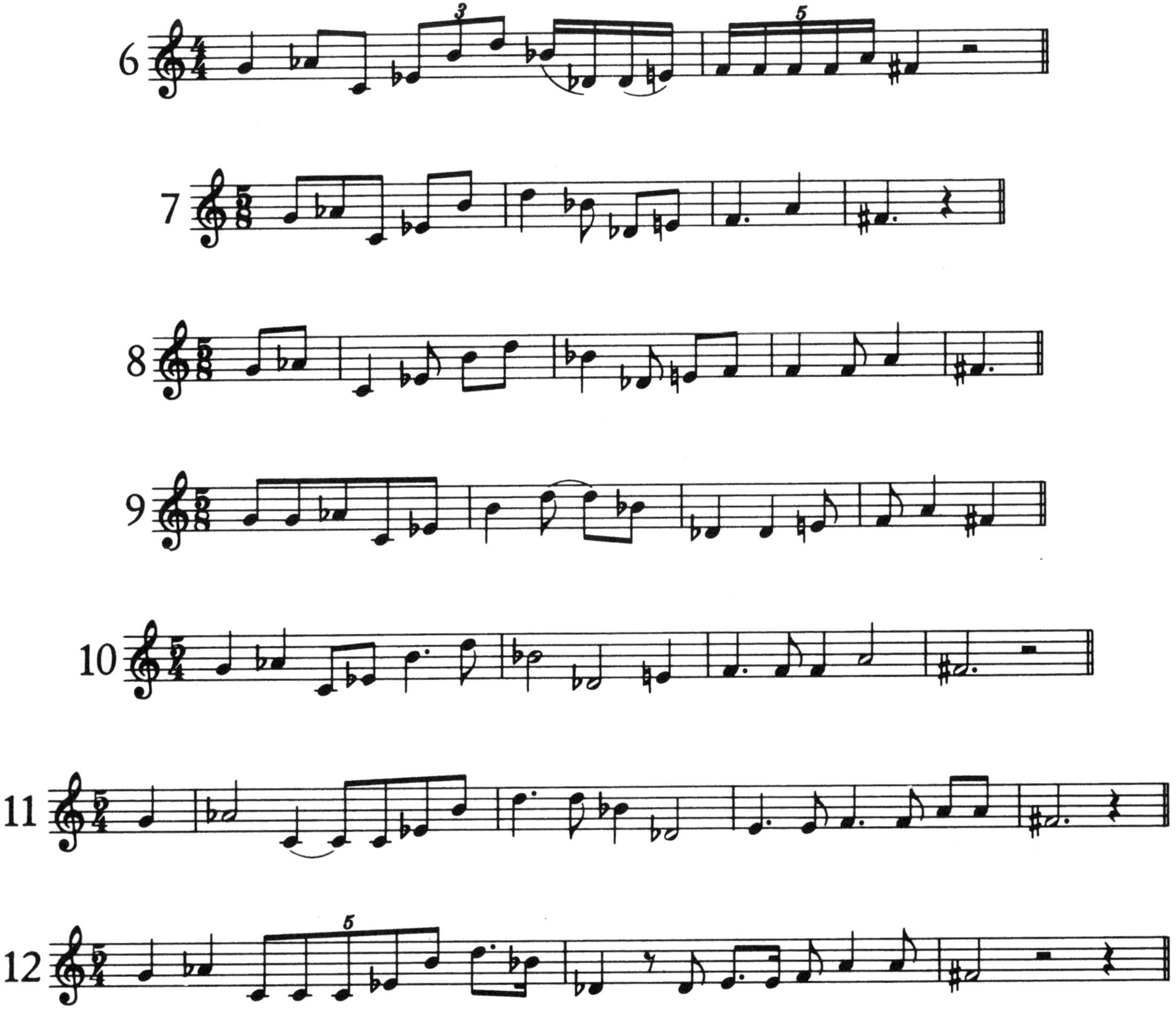
6
7
8
9
10
11
12

FIGURED BASS EXERCISES

The figured bass exercises have the following purposes:

1) DICTATION: The teacher should play *realized* versions of the figured bass examples from the appendix containing the *figured* bass parts (page 208). The student should analyze the chords aurally and write the figurations for the examples in the book.

2) KEYBOARD EXERCISES: The examples dictated during the lesson should be given as homework for the student to realize on the piano at the next lesson.

These exercises not only effectively develop an ability to listen and think in harmonic terms, but they also develop proficiency in using the principal major/minor chords at the piano. Together with the harmonic exercises on pages 193 - 202, the Figured Bass Exercises give many opportunities to improvise freely and play by ear.

REQUIREMENTS:
Performance of these exercises requires

1) the teacher to be able to realize the figured examples which are found in the appendix.
2) the student already to be able to read figured bass symbols, or else he will have to learn as he goes along.
3) the student to be able to play these exercises on the piano and to have familiarity with the classical conventions governing the movement of voices in four-part harmony.

The subject of figured bass only has been briefly touched upon, since its scope is beyond the aims of this book. Students wishing to acquire knowledge of the fundamentals of figured bass theory are referred to other literature! [1]

---

[1] For example, Keller: **Thorough Bass Method,** Norton. For the study of more advanced figured bass playing, see Rob. Donington: **The Interpretation of Early Music,** London 1963, and F.T. Arnold: **The Art of Accompaniment from a Thorough-Bass,** London 1931, 1961.

GENERAL DIRECTIONS:
Here is a brief outline of the most common figured bass symbols.

The figures show the intervals in each chord, starting from the *bass note* going upwards.

These differ from the chord symbols, which are determined by the root of the chords and their function in a particular harmonic context. The figured bass symbols say nothing about this context or the function of the chords in relation to other chords. The number 7 below a bass note does not necessarily mean a dominant seventh chord. This will depend on whether or not the bass note in question is the dominant of the key in which the music is written (or is in at that particular moment).

1. All figures indicate intervals formed from notes found *within the key*. If an interval is to be raised or lowered, this is indicated by $\sharp$, b, or $\natural$ beside the number in question. The augmentation of an interval can also be indicated by a figure with a +: $6+, 4+, 2+, {}^{6}_{3}\sharp$

2. An accidental by itself without a figure always refers to the third of the chord.

3. A note without a figure indicates a triad in root position.

4. The number 6 (or $^6_3$) means a chord in first inversion (six chord).

Note :

Certain figures in the symbols often are omitted, just as they are in the actual designations of the chords. We usually say "six-five chord", not "six-five-three chord". But if one of the intervals in the chord is changed chromatically, then the corresponding figure must appear together with its appropriate accidental.

5. $^6_4$ = means a six-four chord
6. 7 (or $^7_5$ or $^7_5_3$) means a seventh chord
7. $^6_5$ (or $^6_5_3$) means a six-five chord

8. $\begin{smallmatrix}4\\3\end{smallmatrix}$ (or $\begin{smallmatrix}6\\4\\3\end{smallmatrix}$) means a four-three chord

9. 2 (or $\begin{smallmatrix}4\\2\end{smallmatrix}$ or $\begin{smallmatrix}6\\4\\2\end{smallmatrix}$) means a four-two chord

10. Several figures appearing one after the other below the same bass note usually indicate the linear movement of a part. Usually one or more notes will remain stationary. These notes are generally suspensions, neighboring tones, or passing tones. For example:

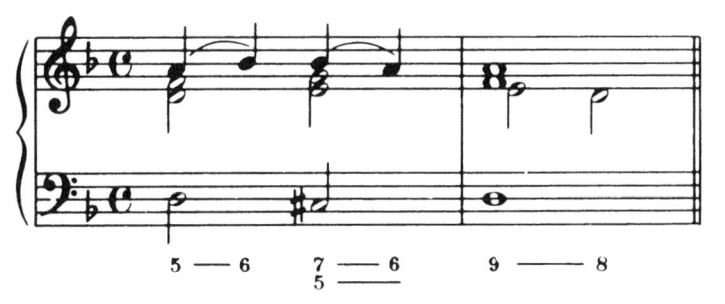

11. Faster bass parts which move chiefly by step often contain unharmonized passing tones, and the chords fall mainly on the accented down beats. In these exercises certain passing tones have been marked with a horizontal line in front of the note.

SOME ADVICE ON USE:

When giving dictation, the teacher should play slowly, play only small sections at a time, and repeat each section as many times as may be required. He also should make sure that the student is certain of the bass note on which the whole figured bass is built. Violinists, flutists, sopranos, and tenors sometimes have difficulty in identifying the bass of a chord. Often it is a good idea to let the student sing the bass of the chord, as well as the complete chords in close position, naming the notes.

When the student plays music incorporating figured bass, he should begin with traditional four-part harmony in close position, with the left hand playing only the bass part. In the author's experience, however, it is wise not to be as strict when the student is playing as when he is writing out the exercise. Psychologically it often helps to ignore consecutive fifths and octaves rather than to inhibit the student's freedom at the keyboard by rigorous demands. One is reminded of the old principle that "since music exists solely for the ear, a "mistake" which does not offend the ear is not a mistake." (Michel de Saint-Lambert' *Nouveau Traite de l'Accompagnement du Clavecin, 1707)*

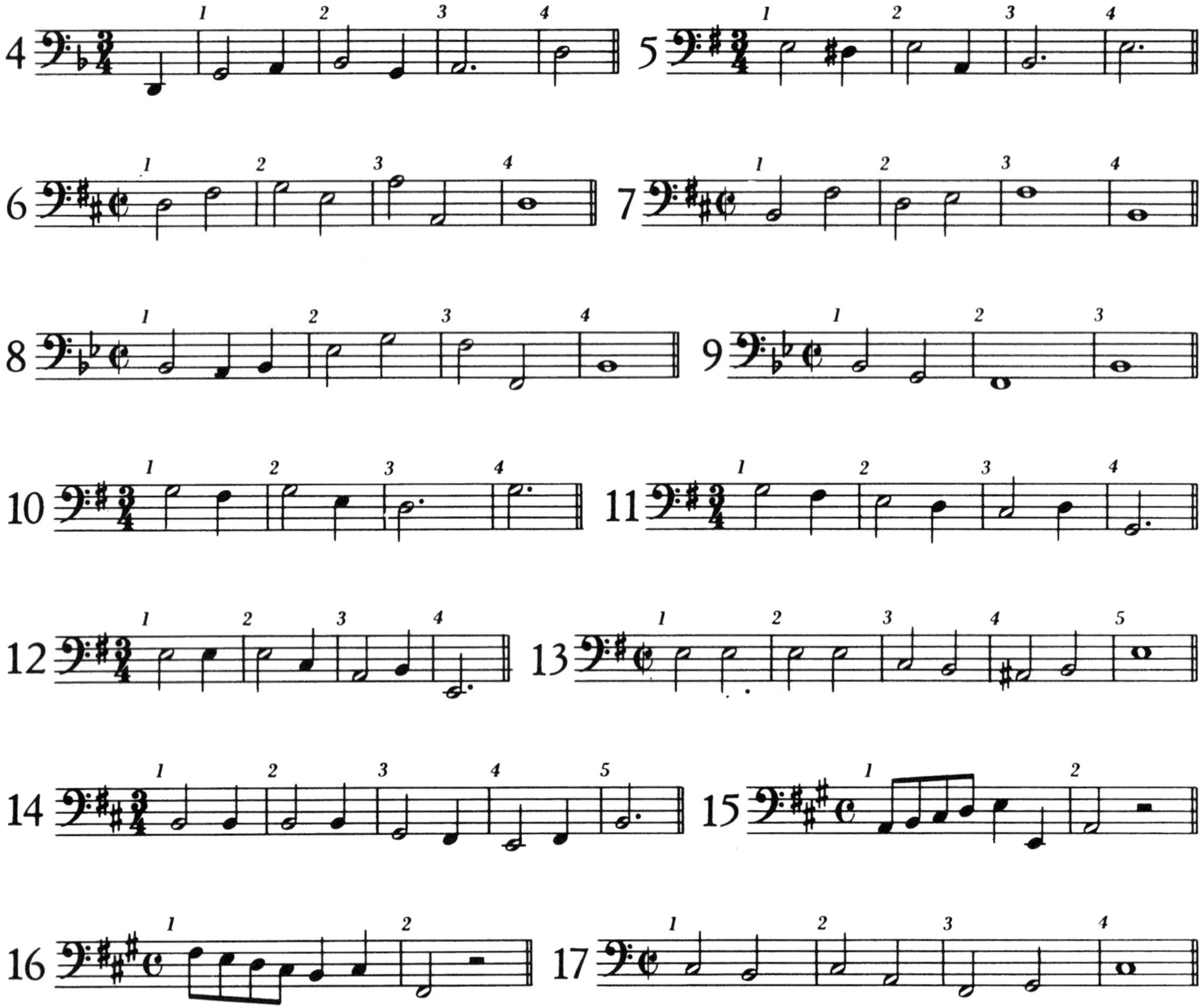

18 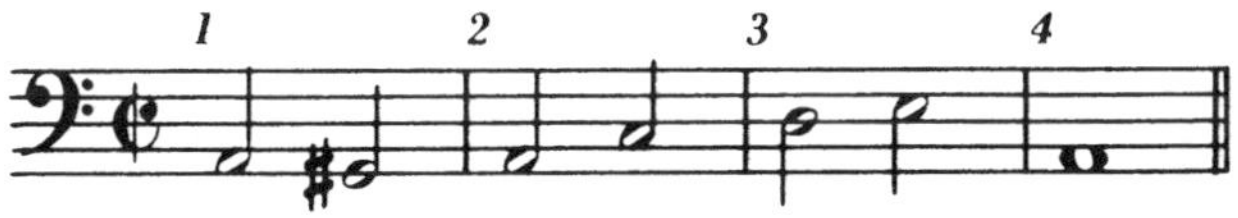

19 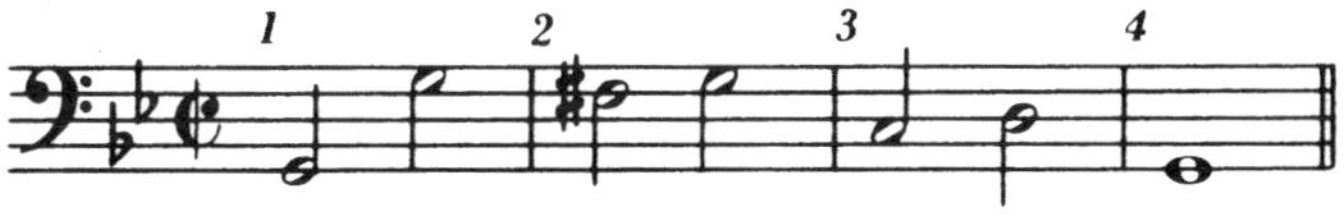

20 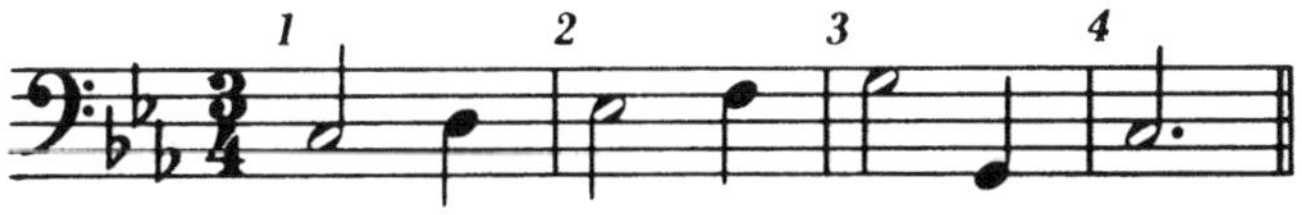

21 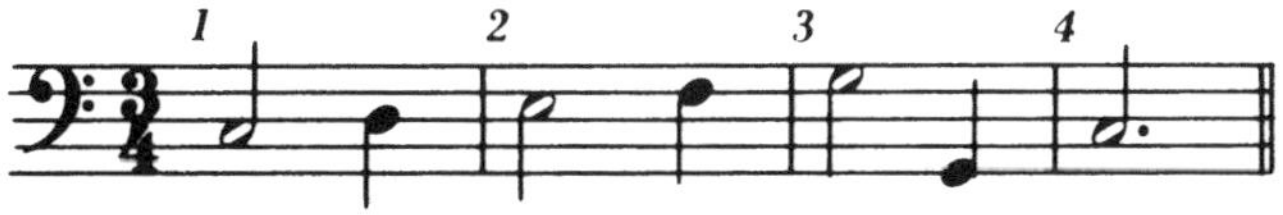

22 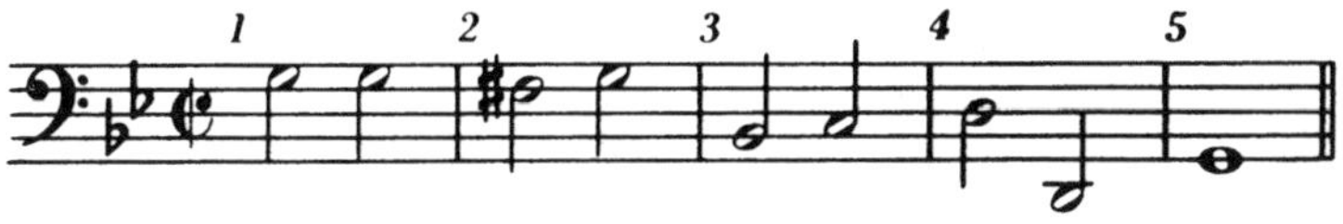

23 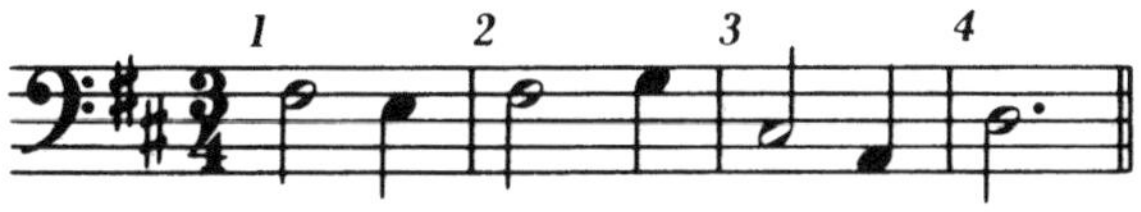

24 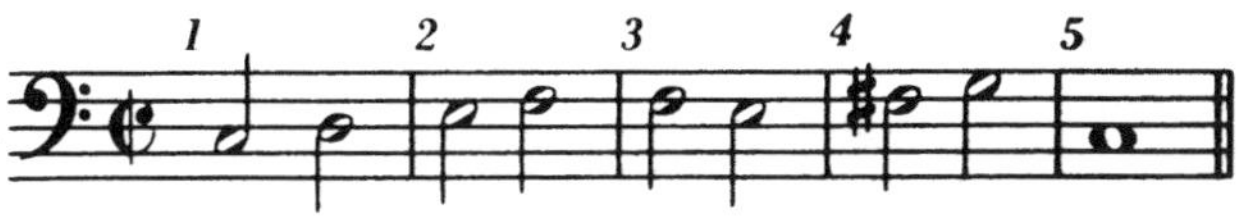

25 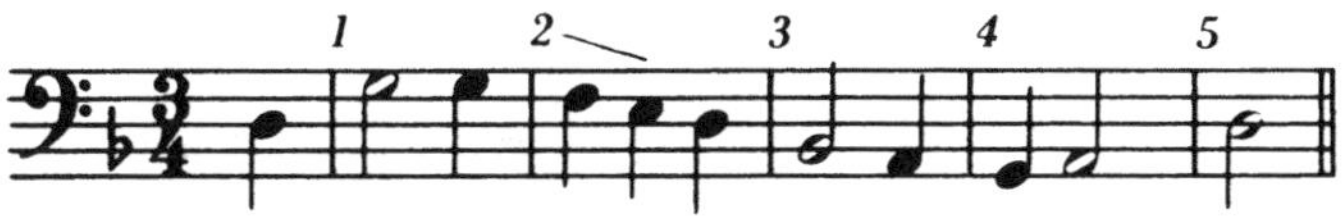

26 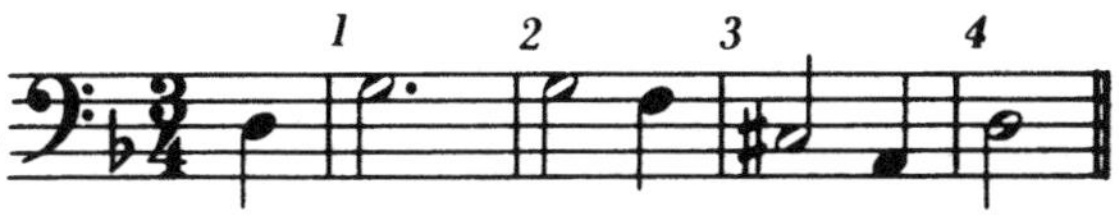

27 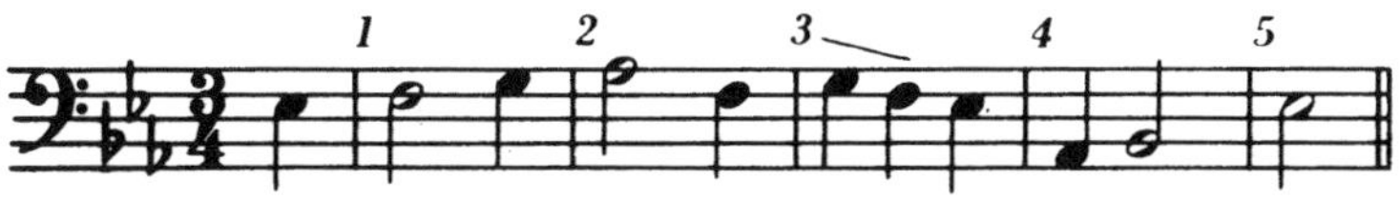

28 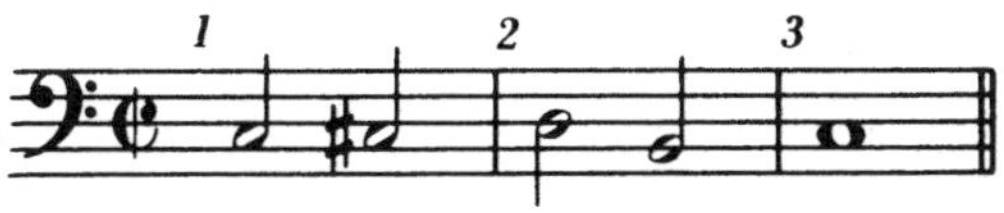

29 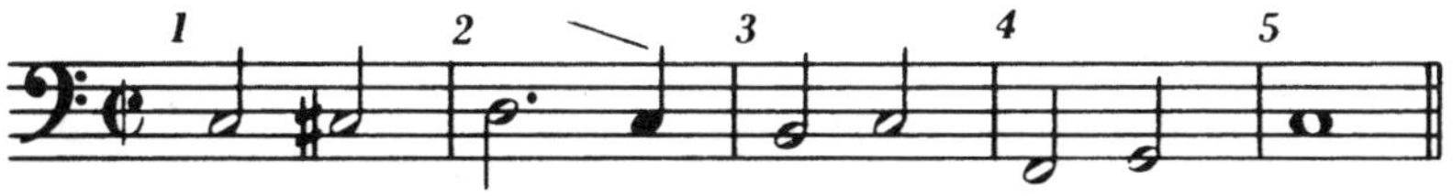

30 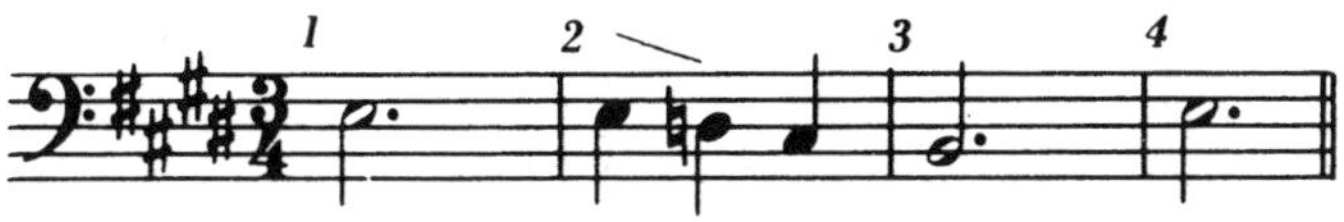

31 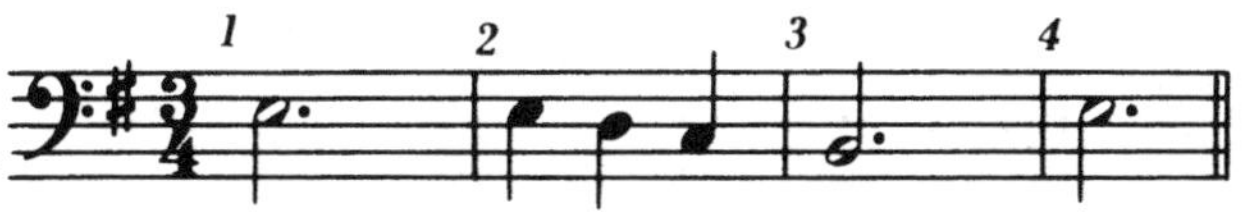

184

39

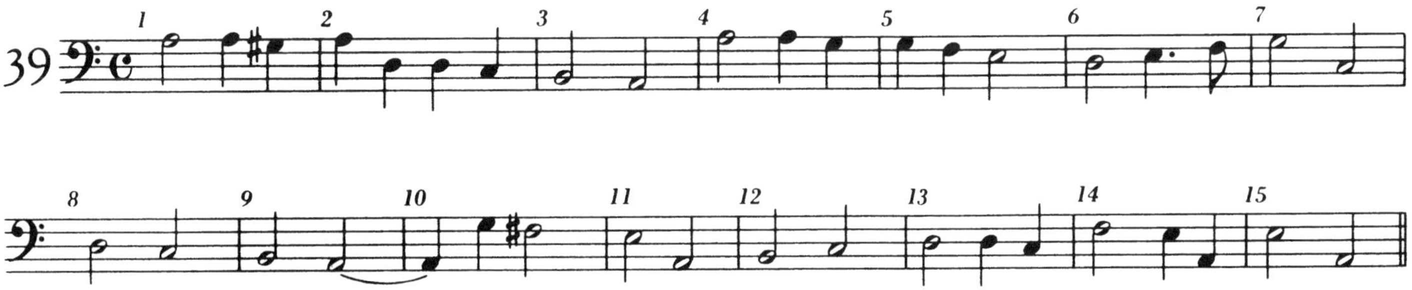

40

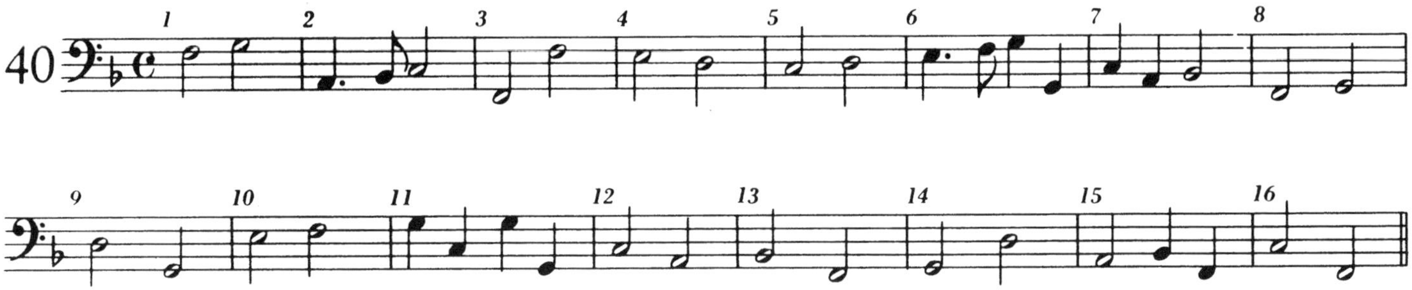

41

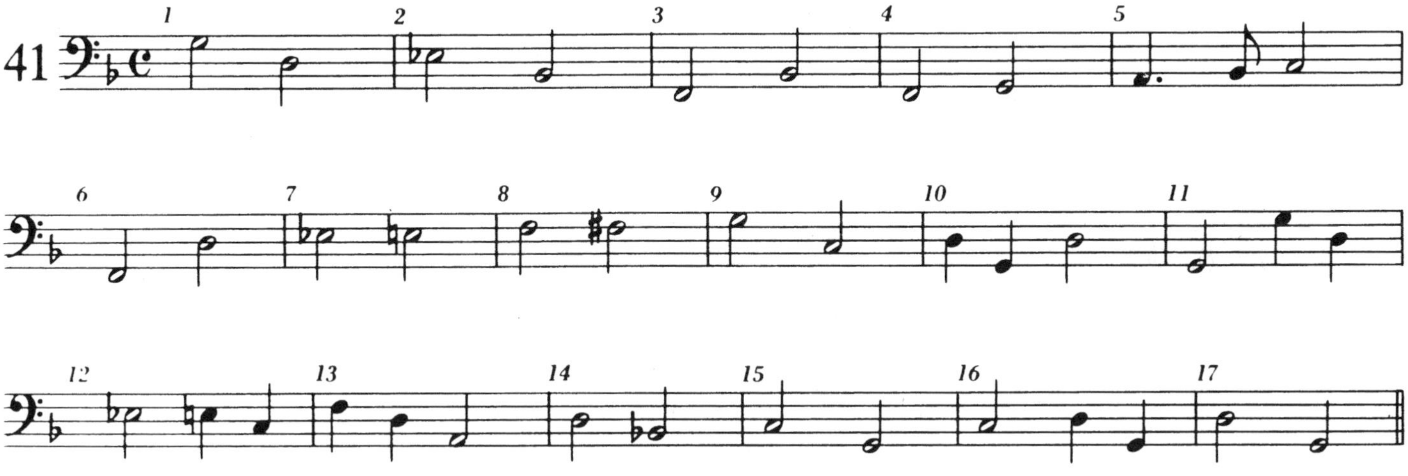

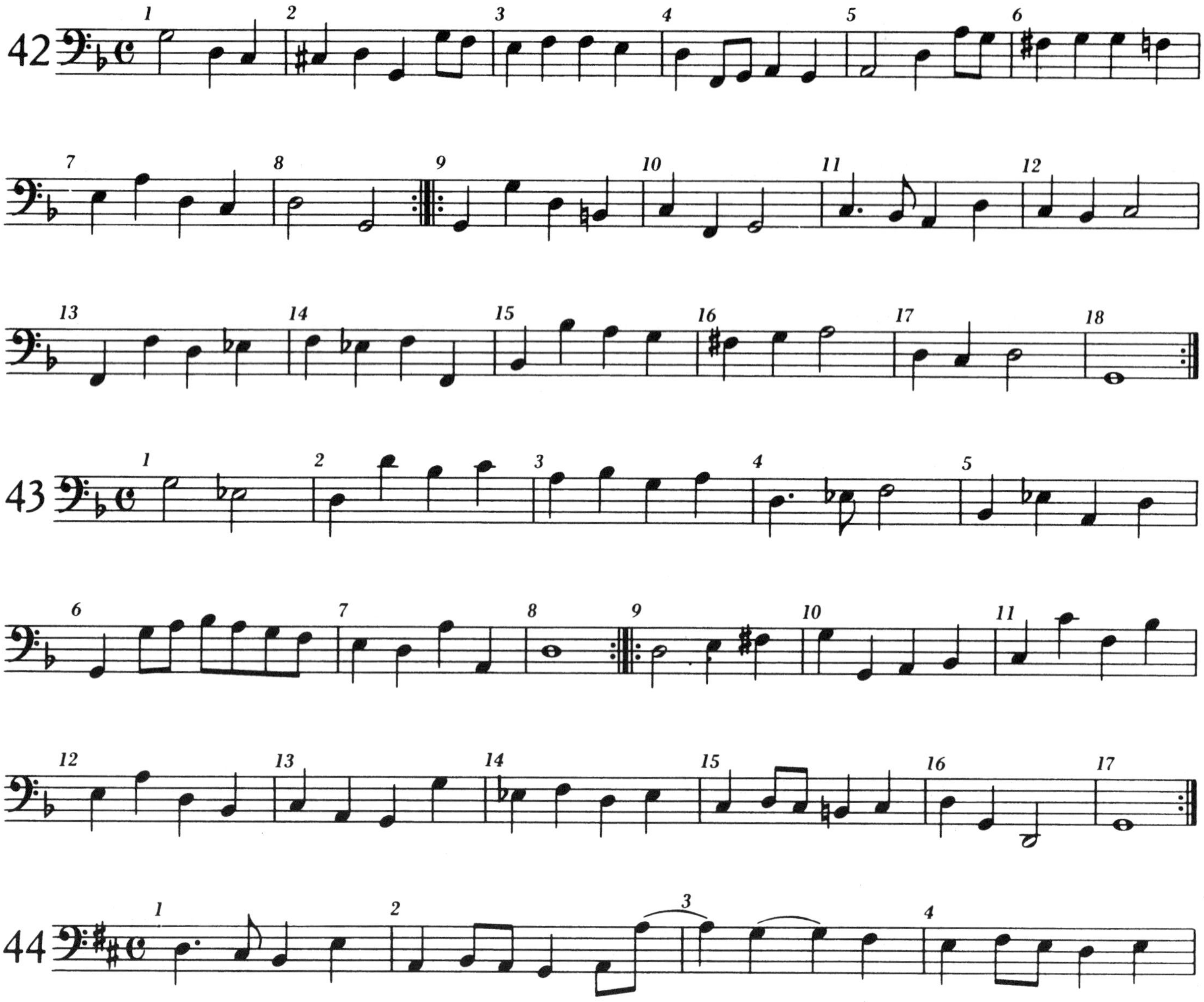
42
43
44

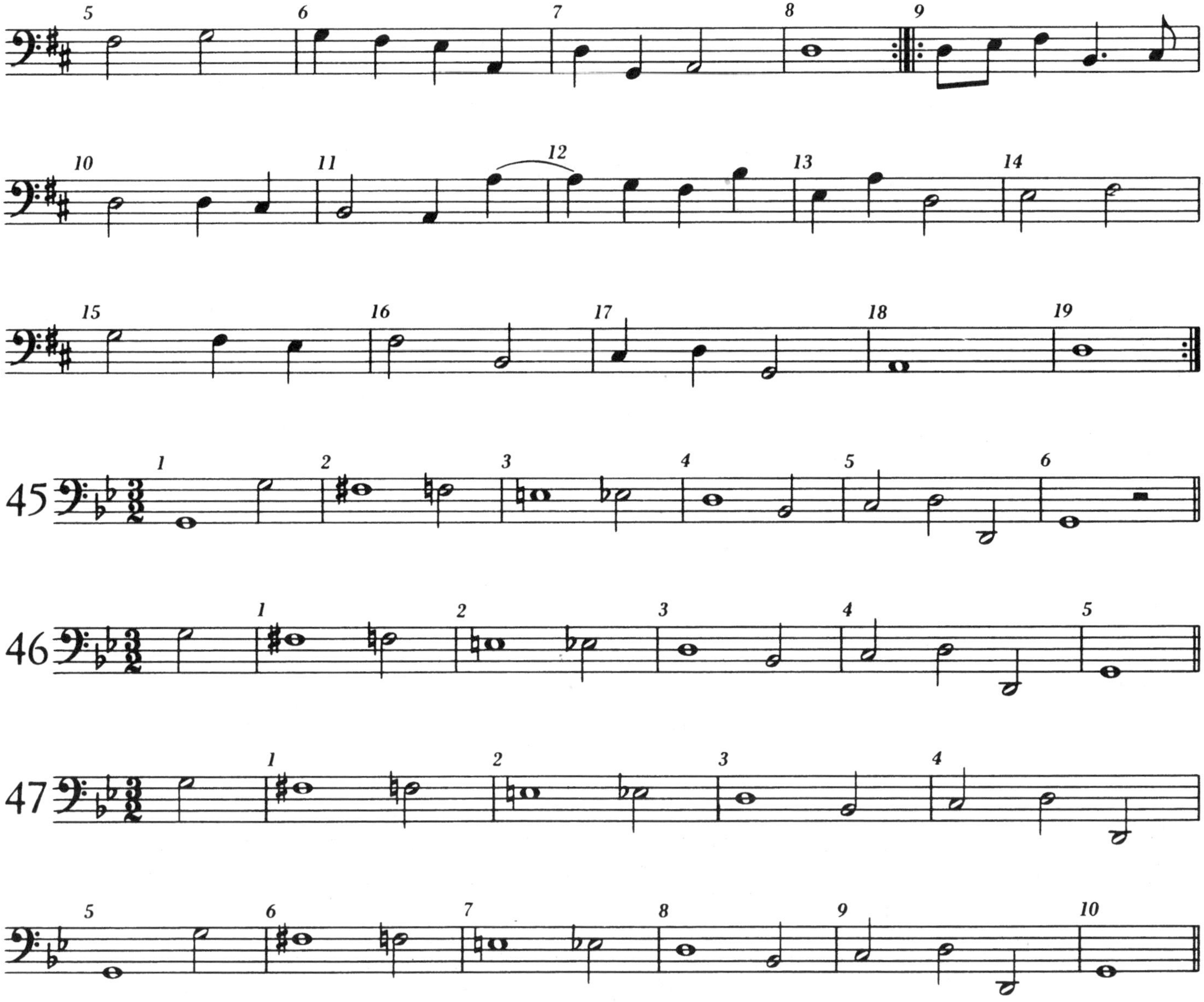
45
46
47

188

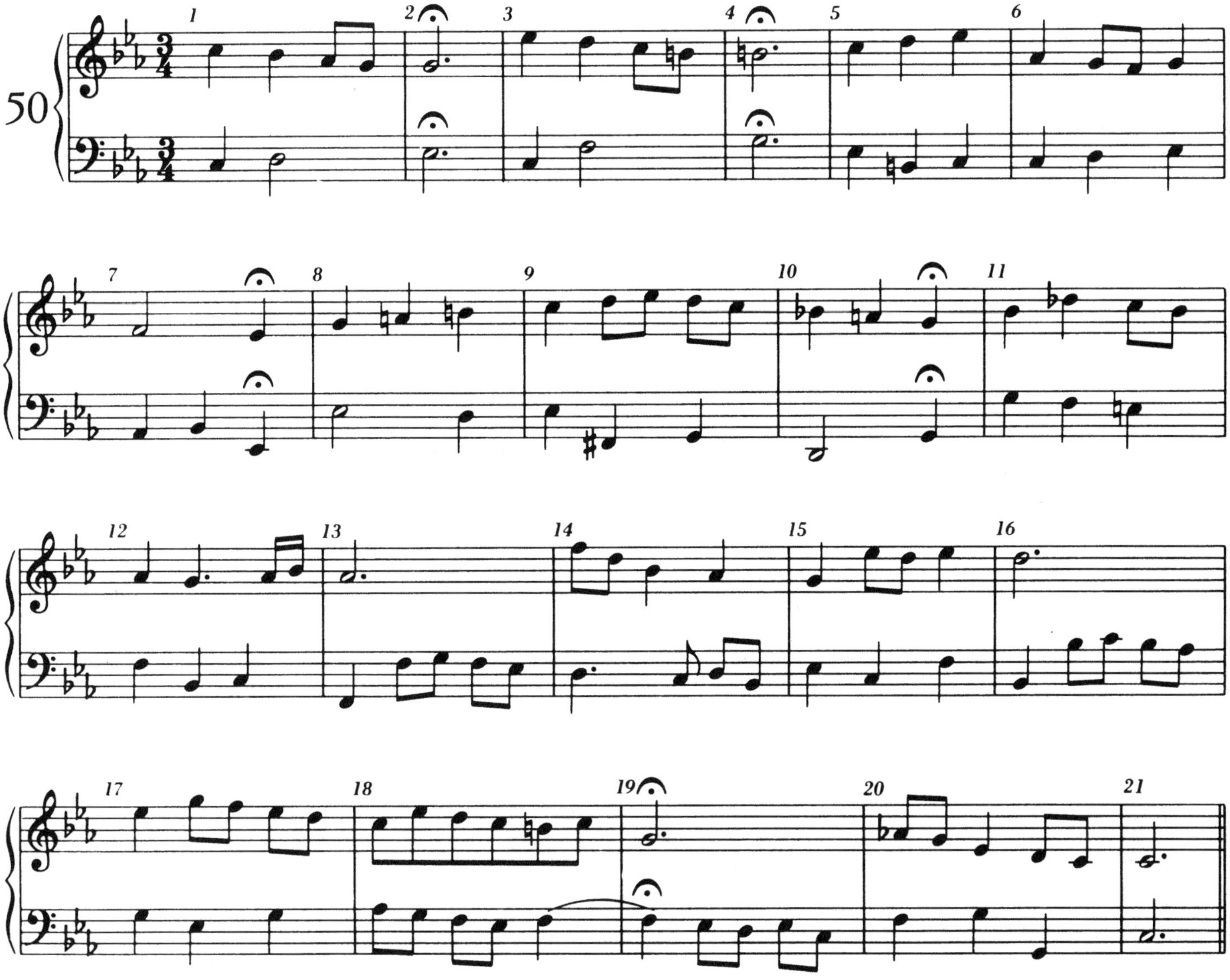
50
1
2
3
4
5
6
7
8
9
10
11
12
13
14
15
16
17
18
19
20
21

190

191

192

KEYBOARD HARMONY EXERCISES

The following material consists of many examples containing various kinds of chords. They cover most of the chordal material encountered in any traditional harmony book. *But this is not a harmony textbook!* Nothing is mentioned here about the movement of parts, the treatment of dissonances, etc. The exercises are suggestions for *keyboard practice* relating to traditional harmony, which often tends to become stereotyped in abstract written exercises. The purpose of these exercises is to have the student play harmonic impulses, either here in the form of chord symbols, or from his own imagination or memory (improvisation, playing tunes, playing excerpts from compositions, etc.).

The second is the more important. Realization from the chord symbols is merely the methodical task which will lead to greater facility on the keyboard using the framework of major/minor tonal harmony. Many people fancy that they have a natural aptitude for playing by ear. Usually they have learned to do this in childhood - perhaps because they had difficulty in learning to read music! Others who depend more on the printed music can, by practice, *improve their playing by ear.* Careful study of the material provided below will prove this fact. This demands a lot of hard work, and the following exercises contain only one of several methods in this type of training. Do not forget the Figured Bass Exercises, page 180, which to a large extent develop the same skills as the exercises in this chapter.

HOW TO PLAY THE EXERCISES:
It is essential for the student to be familiar with the chord symbols and to be able to play the piano well enough to play these exercises. Most students probably will find it difficult to do the exercises without the guidance of a teacher.

As in the Figured Bass Exercises, we take four-part harmony as *a starting point,* but we do not make it the basis of hard and fast rules. These are *keyboard exercises,* not strict choral harmony. Practice three-part harmony frequently, even if the examples are mostly in four parts. You must feel free to change the number of parts. Do not stick to one particular key. The models are written always in the key of C only for the sake of simplicity.

Furthermore, each example should be practiced
a) with the initial chord in different positions.
b) in both close and open positions.
c) in major and minor keys unless otherwise stated.

The relationship between rhythm and harmony is an important aspect of theory. For the special study of this relationship, the student is advised to consult music literature.[1] In the following exercises we merely stress the importance of giving a clear rhythmic outline at the piano so that they do not result in a series of chords of arbitrary duration. They must develop into rhythmic figures which become formal elements to both student and listener (real or imaginary). The rhythms given in the examples on the next page are only suggestions. Duple and triple meters make good basic alternatives. Experimentation should be done in various forms and different tempos. The teacher should be critical of the harmonic/rhythmic relationship.

Finally, the exercises also can be used for chordal dictation. The teacher should play the examples and the pupil should write the chord symbols without notation.

[1] The relationship between rhythm and harmony is treated in, among other sources, Walter Piston: Harmony, Norton.

1. a) $\frac{2}{4}$ I V | I - ‖   b) $\frac{3}{4}$ I - V | I - - ‖

Example:

2. a) $\frac{2}{4}$ I V^6 | I - ‖   b) $\frac{3}{4}$ I - V^6 | I - - ‖

3. $\frac{2}{4}$ I IV | I - ‖   Also in triple meter:

4. $\frac{2}{4}$ I I^6 | IV - | I - ‖   Try also to do the examples using slightly more movement in the melody line.

Example:

5. a) $\frac{4}{4}$ I - IV - | V - I - ‖   b) $\frac{3}{4}$ I | IV - V | I - ‖

6. $\frac{3}{4}$ I - I^6 | IV - V | I - - ‖

7. $\frac{4}{4}$ I - V^6 V | I - I^6 | IV - V - | I — ‖

Example:

8. $\frac{3}{4}$ V⁶ | I I⁶ I | IV - - | I - ‖

Example:

9. a) $\frac{2}{4}$ I IV⁶ | I - ‖   b) $\frac{4}{4}$ I - IV⁶ IV | V - I - ‖

Example: a)   b)

10. $\frac{3}{4}$ I I⁶ IV | I⁶₄ - V | I - - ‖

Example:

11. $\frac{3}{4}$ I - IV⁶ | I⁶₄ - V | I - - ‖

12. $\frac{2}{4}$ I V^7 | I - ‖

13. $\frac{2}{4}$ I V$^6_5$ | T - ‖

14. $\frac{2}{4}$ I V$^4_3$ | I^6 IV | I$^6_4$ - V | I - ‖
    or VII^6

Example:

15. $\frac{2}{4}$ I I^6 | IV V$^4_2$ | I^6 V^6 $^6_5$ | I - ‖

Example:

16. $\frac{3}{4}$ I | II^7_b - V | I ‖   Note: Don't forget that a minor subdominant (here IV$^6_5$) can occur in a major key and a major subdominant in a minor key. Practice both!

17. $\frac{3}{4}$ I | II$^5_6$ - V^7 | I - ‖

Example:

18. $\frac{3}{4}$ I | II$^6_2$ - V$^6_5$ | I - ‖

Example:

19. $\frac{3}{4}$ I | II$^{7}_{(b)}$ - V$^{4}_{3}$ | I - || Example:

20. $\frac{3}{4}$ I | II$^{6}_{5\,(b)}$ V | I - || Example:

21. $\frac{3}{4}$ I(b) | II$^{6\,b}_{b}$ - V | I - || Example:
    or
    I(b) | N^{6} - V | I - ||

    II$^{6\,b}_{b}$ or N^{6} means a Neapolitan sixth chord.

22. $\frac{2}{4}$ I V^{o7b} | I - || Example:

23. $\frac{2}{4}$ I V$^{06}_{5\flat}$| I^6 ... Finish the example and end with the tonic in root position.

24. $\frac{3}{4}$ I |IV - V$^{04}_{\flat}$| I^3 ... Finish it yourself!

25. $\frac{3}{4}$ I |IV^6 V^{02}| I$^6_4$ ... Finish it yourself!

26. $\frac{3}{4}$ I - I^6 |V/V - V^6| I - V^7 | I - - ‖

27. $\frac{3}{4}$ I |IV^6 I$^6_4$|V^6/V - V| I - ‖

28. $\frac{3}{4}$ I - V^7/ V| V$^{8-7}$ | I - - ‖

29. $\frac{3}{4}$ I - V$^6_5$/ V| V$^{4-3}$ | I - - ‖

30. $\frac{3}{4}$ I - V$^4_3$/ V| V$^{7-}_{4-3}$ | I - - ‖

31. $^3_4\text{I} - \text{V}^{o6}/\text{V} \mid \text{V}^{4-3} \mid \text{I} - - \parallel$

32. $^3_4\text{I} - \text{V}^{4+}_2/\text{V} \mid \text{V}^6_3 - ^6_5 \mid \text{I} - - \parallel$

In the following examples the student must complete the exercises first by creating a good beginning, then by playing the given harmonic progression, and finally by completing them in a suitable manner.

33. .... $\text{V}^{o7\flat}/\text{V} \mid \text{V}$ .... 34. .... $\text{V}^{o6}_5/\text{V} \mid \text{V}^6$ ....

35. .... $\text{V}^{o4}_3/\text{V} \mid \text{V}^6$ .... 36. .... $\text{V}^{o4}_2/\text{V} \mid \text{V}^4_3$ ....

37. The secondary dominant or applied dominant, $\text{V}^7/\text{V} - \text{IV}$, should be practiced in the following versions:

    a) .... $\text{V}^7/\text{IV} \mid \text{IV}$ .... b) .... $\text{V}^6_5/\text{IV} \mid \text{IV}$ ....

    c) .... $\text{V}^4_3/\text{IV} \mid \text{IV}$ .... d) .... $\text{V}^{o2}/\text{IV} \mid \text{IV}^6$ ....

    e) .... $\text{V}^{o7}_{5\,(\flat)}{}^{\flat}/\text{IV} \mid \text{IV}$ .... f) .... $\text{V}^{o6}_{5\,(\flat)}{}^{(+)}/\text{IV} \mid \text{IV}$ ....

    g) .... $\text{V}^{o4}_{3\flat}/\text{IV} \mid \text{IV}^6$ ....

38. The following cadence [1] contains these additional chords of the major key: mediant, submediant, and supertonic. The cadence should be practiced in all major keys. Practice both close and open positions in various ways.

[1] Used by Anton Bruckner in his harmony teaching.

      I   III   VI IV   II   V   I

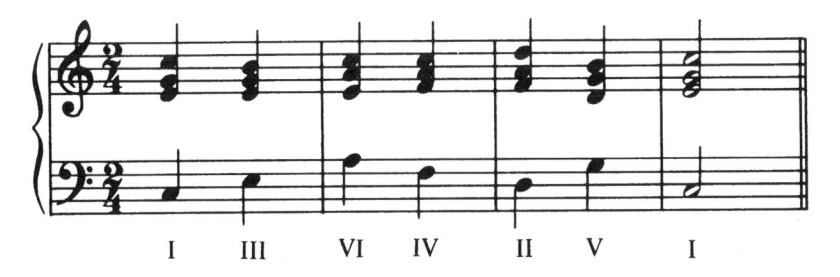

39. In the following cadence practice the same chords in the parallel minor key. Carefully study the chords which differ from those in the major key. The cadence is to be practiced using the same principles stated in exercise 38.

      I   VII   III   V   VI   IV   V♯   I

40. Practice the secondary dominant to supertonic of the related major, V/II - II, in all major keys. The secondary dominant should be practiced in the following versions:

   a) .... V/II | II ....   b) .... V^6/II | II ....

   c) .... V^7/II | II ....   d) .... V^6_5/II | II ....

   e) .... V^4_3/II | II ....   f) .... V^2/II | II ....

   g) .... V^{o9}/II | II ....   h) .... V^{o6}_5/II | II^6 ....

   i) .... V^{o4}_3/II | II^6 ....

41. Practice the secondary dominant to submediant, V/VI - VI, in all major keys. The secondary dominant should be practiced in the same versions used in exercise 40.

42. Practice V/VI - III in all major keys. Here also the secondary dominant should be practiced in the same versions used in exercise 40.

43. The secondary dominant to primary and secondary chords of the minor key should be practiced using the same principles as shown above for the major key.

44. Practice modulation to the keys temporarily affected by the above secondary dominants to various primary and secondary chords. Do not lead the examples back to the original key, but complete them in the key to which the secondary dominant has temporarily led, thus becoming the dominant of the new key.

45. Let us conclude this series of keyboard harmony exercises by practicing different resolutions of the diminished seventh (V^{o9}). It has been encountered previously in connection with melody reading, page 124. There it was pointed out that this chord, which consists of three minor thirds piled one on top of the other, contains strong leading tone tendencies. This is partly true because it also contains two diminished fifths and no perfect fifth.

Suppose you hear a diminished seventh without seeing it notated. It is impossible to say for certain into which key the chord will resolve, since each of the four chordal notes can act as the leading tone of the resolution key, or the third in the V^{o9} chord. (Refer to the explanation on page 126). In other words, we do not know whether we hear a V^{o9}, V^{o5}_{5}, V^{o4}_{3}, or a V^{o2} chord.

The examples below will demonstrate this clearly. Play the chords in the right hand and let them sound for a few moments before playing the "omitted" bass note in the left hand. Notice how clearly the bass note stabilizes the tonality and governs the resolution. When the bass note is added, the other notes in the chord acquire a definite function. The leading tone with its resolution has been marked with an arrow.

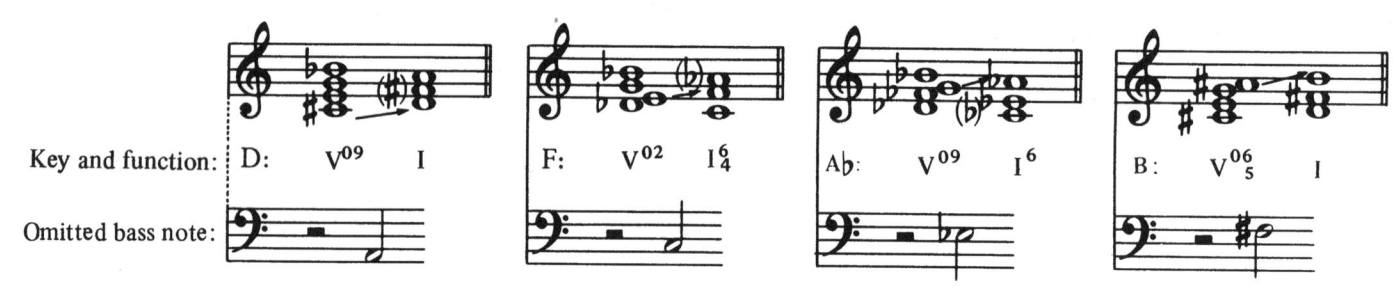

Key and function: D: V^{o9} I   F: V^{o2} I^6_4 A♭: V^{o9} I^6 B: V^{o6}_{5} I

Omitted bass note:

EXERCISE: Practice these four different alternatives for resolution using the following two diminished sevenths:

Because of its ambiguity this chord is useful for purposes of modulation. Stylistically such modulations belong chiefly to a somewhat chromaticized major/minor tonality as used by the late Romantics Liszt, Wagner, Reger, and Mahler.

EXERCISE: Practice modulations using the V^{o9} chord as the means of modulation.

HARMONIC EXERCISES IN CONNECTION WITH THE MELODIES SUGGESTED METHOD

The skills which have been acquired through practice in keyboard harmony, page 193, also can be applied to harmonic exercises in melody reading. This can be done by using the following method after the student has sung the melody. (Melody for demonstration purposes - No. 9, page 9).

The teacher should play the melody harmonized very simply. (See also 1 and 2 below. Notice: Only chords from sections 1 and 2 of the Keyboard Harmony Exercises are used!) Possibly only the melody and the bass parts should be played. The teacher should not harmonize each melody note with its own separate chord. This type of harmonization is often rhythmically very heavy. Allow various notes to be passing tones, neighboring tones, etc.

The student should notate the bass line and identify the harmonic function of each note. Later these should be written in pencil under the notes.

The student should sing the bass line, namine the notes from the fraction symbols. Perhaps first he should read the names of the notes.

The student should sing the bass line while the teacher or another student sings the melody.

The student should sing the melody and play the bass line on the piano at the same time.

The student should play the melody and the bass line on the piano. This can be done even by students whose basic instrument is not the piano. Students with greater facility naturally should practice more than just the melody and bass line. One may notice that here it often is better to have too few tones in the chords than too many. In these exercises we are not searching for traditional four-part writing. The teacher may choose a number of melodies from each chapter for that type of exercise. The progressions used should follow principally those in the Keyboard Harmony Exercises. See the table above on page 6.

Sources of melodies in Melody Reading Exercises

Melodies not included in this list have been composed by the author.

The Swedish folksongs are taken mostly from *Sture Bergel - Musikkommentar till Geijer-Afzelius: Svenska Folkvisor*, Stockholm, 1960. Most of the melodies in Chapter XV are taken from *Europäische Lieder in den Ursprachen, Berlin, 1956*.

Chapter VI

- 13 J.S. Bach: Fugue in E major (Well-Tempered Clavier II)
- 14 R. Schumann: Dichterliebe
- 15 J. Brahms: Haydn variations
- 35 A. Striggio: Il cicalamento delle donne al bucato

Chapter VII

- 19 J.S. Bach: Fugue in C minor, Well-Tempered Clavier I

Chapter X

- 4 J.S. Bach: Fugue in C major, Organ Works, vol. VII
- 5 J.S. Bach: Fugue in C major, Organ Works, vol. II
- 6 L. van Beethoven: String quartet in E minor, op. 59 No. 2
- 8 Melchior Franck: Da pacem (Canon).
- 10 L. van Beethoven: Symphony No. 2 in D major
- 15 J.S. Bach: Fugue in C major, Well-Tempered Clavier I
- 17 J.S. Bach: Fugue in E major, Well-Tempered Clavier II
- 18 W.A. Mozart: Symphony in G minor, K. 550
- 20 B. Bartok: For children
- 21 F. Schubert: Die Winterreise
- 22 J. Sibelius: Finlandia
- 23 Carl Nielsen: Piano music for young and old
- 24 J.S. Bach: Fugue in F. major, Well-Tempered Clavier I
- 25 J.S. Bach: Fugue in C major, Well-Tempered Clavier II
- 26 I. Stravinsky: The Firebird
- 27 W.A. Mozart: The Magic Flute
- 29 R. Schumann: Dichterliebe
- 30 Swedish Hymnal No. 35
- 31 L. van Beethoven: String quartet in C major, op. 59 No. 3
- 32 W.A. Mozart: Symphony in D major, K. 385 (Haffner)
- 33 A. Striggio: Il cicalamento
- 34 Swedish folk tune (Dalarna)
- 35 J. Haydn: Symphony No. 94 in G major (Surprise)
- 36 J. Haydn: String quartet in B major, op. 76 No. 4
- 37 R. Schumann: Frauenliebe und Leben
- 38 L. van Beethoven: Symphony No. 2 in D major
     F. Schubert: Die Winterreise

Chapter XI

- 1 Swedish popular melody
- 6 Swedish folk song
- 8 French carol
- 12 J.S. Bach: Art of the Fugue
- 13 J.S. Bach: Fugue in E minor, Well-Tempered Clavier I
- 15 Swedish folk song
- 19 J.S. Bach: Fugue in D minor, Well-Tempered Clavier I
- 20 J.S. Bach: Fugue in G minor, Well-Tempered Clavier I
- 25 A. Krieger: Chorale
- 26 R. Schumann: Liederkreis, op. 39
- 30 W.F. Bach: Sinfonia in D minor
- 31 J.S. Bach: Fugue in F minor, Well-Tempered Clavier II
- 37 J.S. Bach: Fugue in G minor, Well-Tempered Clavier II
- 38 J.S. Bach: Fugue in B minor, Well-Tempered Clavier II
- 39 J.S. Bach: Art of the Fugue
- 40 F. Schubert: Die Winterreise
- 41 J.S. Bach: Fugue in F minor, Well-Tempered Clavier I
- 42 Hymn, Middle Ages
- 43 Antiphon, Middle Ages
- 44 Hymn, Middle Ages
- 45 Graduale Romanum: Mass XI
- 46-49 French carols
- 50-53 I. Stravinsky: Les Noces
- 54-56 I. Stravinsky: Rite of Spring

Chapter XIII

1	J. Brahms: Symphony No. 1 in C minor
9	P. Tchaikovsky: String quartet in D manor, op. 11
11	J.S. Bach: St. Matthew Passion
12	J.S. Bach: Fugue in B major, Organ Works, vol. VIII
13	English nursery rhyme
14	R. Schumann: Dichterliebe
15	G.F. Händel: Messiah
16	W.A. Mozart: String quartet in E major, K. 428
17	W.A. Mozart: String quartet in D major, K. 575
18	W.A. Mozart: String quartet in D major, K. 575
19	W.A. Mozart: Symphony in D major, K. 385 (Haffner)
20	J.S. Bach: Sonata I, Organ Works, vol. I
21	J. Haydn: Symphony No. 94 in G major
22	H. Purcell: Fancy No. 4
23	J.S. Bach: Sonata III, Organ Works, vol. I
24	L. van Beethoven: Violin concerto
25	W.A. Mozart: Violin sonata in A major, K. 305
26	W.A. Mozart: Eine kleine Nachtmusik
27	English nursery rhyme
28	Swedish-Finnish folk song
29	C.M. Bellman: Fredman's songs
30	A. Söderman: The Wedding at Ulfåsa
31-33	Swedish folk song
34	W.A. Mozart: Violin sonata in B major, K. 454
35	L. van Beethoven: String quartet in E major, op. 127
36	L. van Beethoven: String quartet in B major, op. 18, No. 6
37	F. Schubert: Piano sonata in D major, op. 53
40	G.F. Händel: Acis and Galathea
43	J.S. Bach: Wachet auf, Organ Works, vol. VII (Cantata 14)
44	L. van Beethoven: String quartet in B major, op. 130
45	W.A. Mozart: Violin sonata in F major, K. 547
46	J.S. Bach: St. John Passion
47-48	Franz Berwald: Estrella di Soria
49	J.A. Lindblad: Near
50	J.S. Bach: St. John Passion
51-54	J.S. Bach: St. Matthew Passion
55	J.S. Bach: St. John Passion

Chapter XIV

2	L. van Beethoven: String quartet in F minor, op. 95
11	Tor Aulin: Four watercolors for violin and piano
13-14	L. van Beethoven: String quartet in C minor, op. 131
16-17	F. Schubert: Die Winterreise
18	Swedish folk song
19	L. van Beethoven: String quartet in C major, op. 59, No. 3
20	Swedish folk song
21	L. van Beethoven: String quartet in A minor, op. 132
22	G.F. Händel: Messiah
23-24	Swedish folk song
25	Danish folk song
26-28	Swedish folk song
29	G.F. Händel: Piano suite XV
30	Fr. Chopin: Mazurka op. 59
31	Fr. Chopin: Mazurka op. 67, No. 4
32	J.S. Bach: Fugue in C minor, Well-Tempered Clavier I
33	J.S. Bach: Fugue in E minor, Well-Tempered Clavier II
34	J.S. Bach: Fugue in F minor, Well-Tempered Clavier II
35	J.S. Bach: Fugue in E minor, Well-Tempered Clavier I
37	Swedish folk song
38	J.S. Bach: Fugue in D minor, Well-Tempered Clavier II
39-40	J.S. Bach: Art of the Fugue
41	J.S. Bach: Fugue in D minor for piano
42	F. Schubert: Symphony No. 4 in C minor
43	J.S. Bach: Fugue in C minor, Organ Works, vol. II
44-45	Swedish folk song
46	J.A. Lindblad: Confession
47	J.S. Bach: Partita 2 for solo violin
48	J.S. Bach: Fugue in E minor, Organ Works, vol. II
49	J.S. Bach: Sonata 4, Organ Works, vol. I
	J.S. Bach: Jesu, meine Freude, Organ Works, vol. VI

Chapter XV

1. Neidhart von Reuental (c. 1250)
2. Hungary (after Bartok)
3. Turkestan
4. Kasan-Tartar
5. Russia
6. Java
7. North America (Indian)
8. Mongolia
9. Scotland
10. Peru (Indian)
11. Poland
12. Lithuania
13. Croatia
14. Russia
15. Catalania
16. Slovakia
17. Latvia
18. Russia
19. Finland
20. Russia
21. Hungary
22. Lithuania
23. Hungary
24. Poland
25. Ukraine
26. England
27. Russia
28. Russia
29. Lapp melody
30. Serbia
31. Roumania
32. Bulgaria
33. Indonesia
34. Macedonia
35. Armenia

Chapter XVI

1. L. van Beethoven: String quartet in B major, op. 130
2. G.F. Händel: Messiah
3. G. Mahler: Revelge
4. W.A. Mozart: Requiem
5. J. Haydn: String quartet in C major op. 76, No. 3
6. J.S. Bach: Concerto for two violins
15. J. Brahms: German Requiem
16. G.F. Händel: Messiah
17. J.H. Roman: Sinfonia in G major
18. W.A. Mozart: Violin sonata in E major, K. 481
19. Rimsky-Korsakov: Scheherazade
20. J.A. Lindblad: For ever
21-23. J.S. Bach: St. John Passion
24-25. J.S. Bach: St. Matthew Passion

Chapter XVII

1. J. Brahms: German Requiem
2. F. Schubert: Die Winterreise
3. G.F. Händel: Messiah
4. W.A. Mozart: Requiem
5. G.F. Händel: Messiah
6. J.S. Bach: Concerto in D minor for harpsichord
7. G.F. Händel: Messiah
8. J.S. Bach: Partita 2 for solo violin
9. J.S. Bach: Suite 2 for solo violoncello
10. J.S. Bach: St. Matthew Passion
11. W.A. Mozart: Violin sonata in A major, K. 402
12-13. Franz Berwald: Estrella di Soria
14. J.S. Bach: St. Matthew Passion
15-16. J.S. Bach: St. John Passion
17-18. J.S. Bach: St. Matthew Passion
19. C.M. Bellman: Fredman's songs, No. 30
20. Franz Berwald: Estrella di Soria
21-23. W. Stenhammar: Gildet på Solhaug
24. Ture Rangström: The sea is murmuring
25. Ture Rangström: An old dance rhythm
26-27. R. Wagner: Lohengrin
28-35. R. Wagner: Tristan und Isolde

Reference list of figured bass examples

38-44. from J.S. Bach: Grundlicher Unterricht des Generalbasses
45-47. Purcell: Dido and Aeneas
48. J.S. Bach: from Schemellis's Hymnbook: Brunnquell aller Guter
49. J.S. Bach: from Schemellis's Hymnbook: Jesu, meines Herzens Freund
50. J.S. Bach: from Schemellis's Hymnbook: Komm, susser Tod
51. J.S. Bach: from Schemellis's Hymnbook: Kommt Seelen, dieser Tag
52. J.S. Bach: from Schemellis's Hymnbook: So gehst du nun, mein Jesu, hin
53. J.S. Bach: from Schemellis's Hymnbook: Selig wer an Jesu denkt
54. J.S. Bach: from Schemellis's Hymnbook: Mein Jesu, was vor Seelen Weh

Key to Figured Bass Exercises

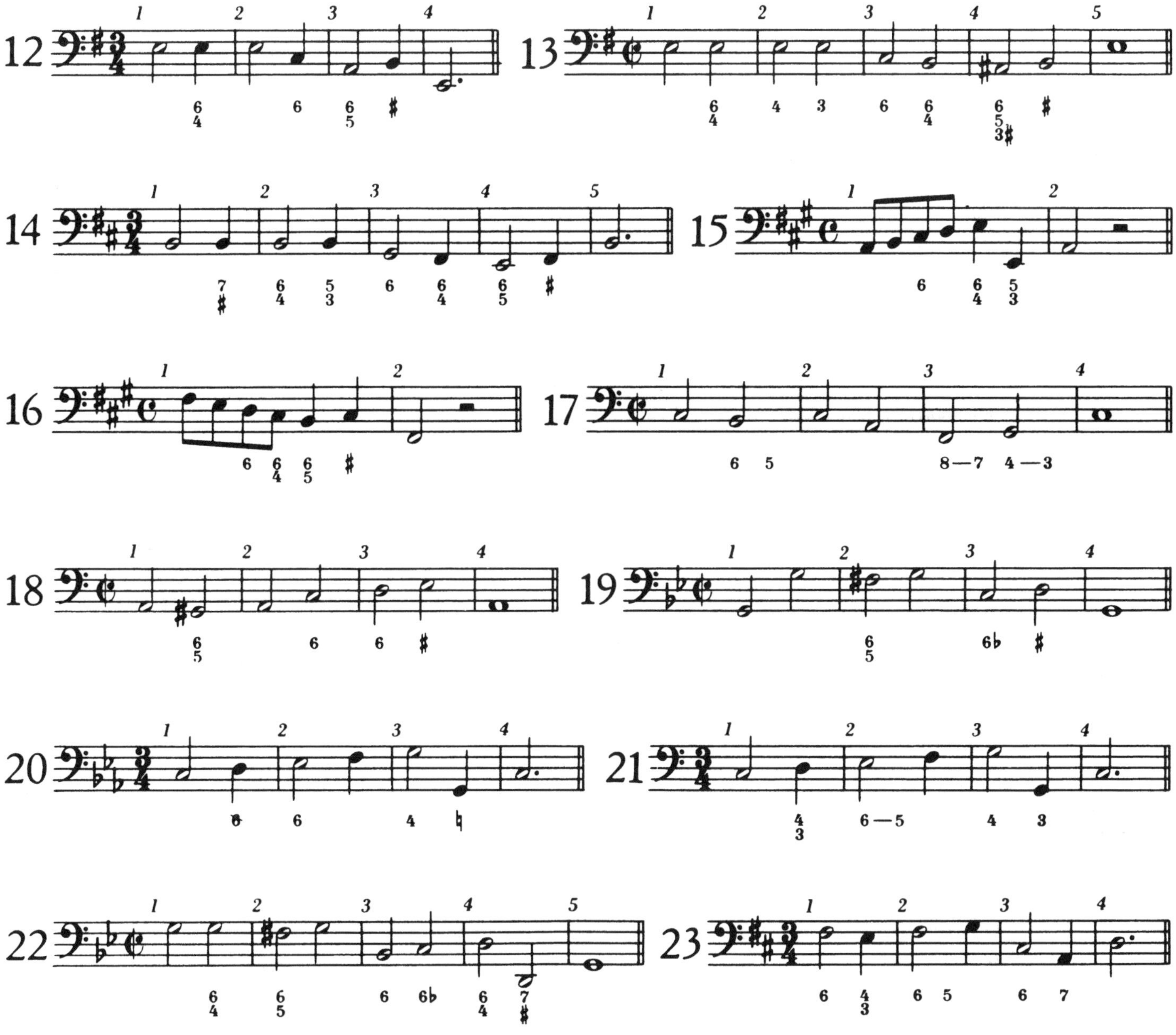

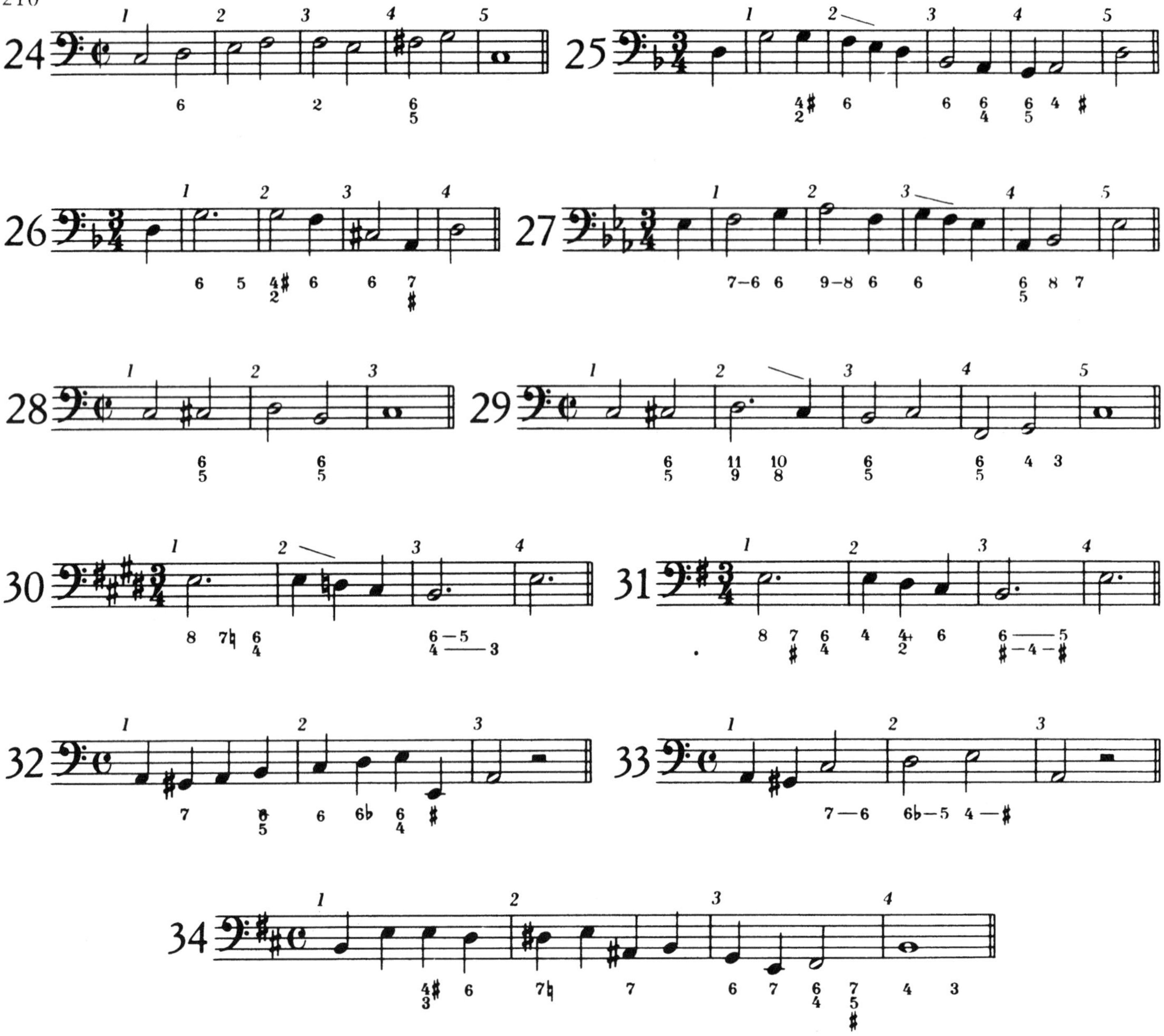
24
25
26
27
28
29
30
31
32
33
34

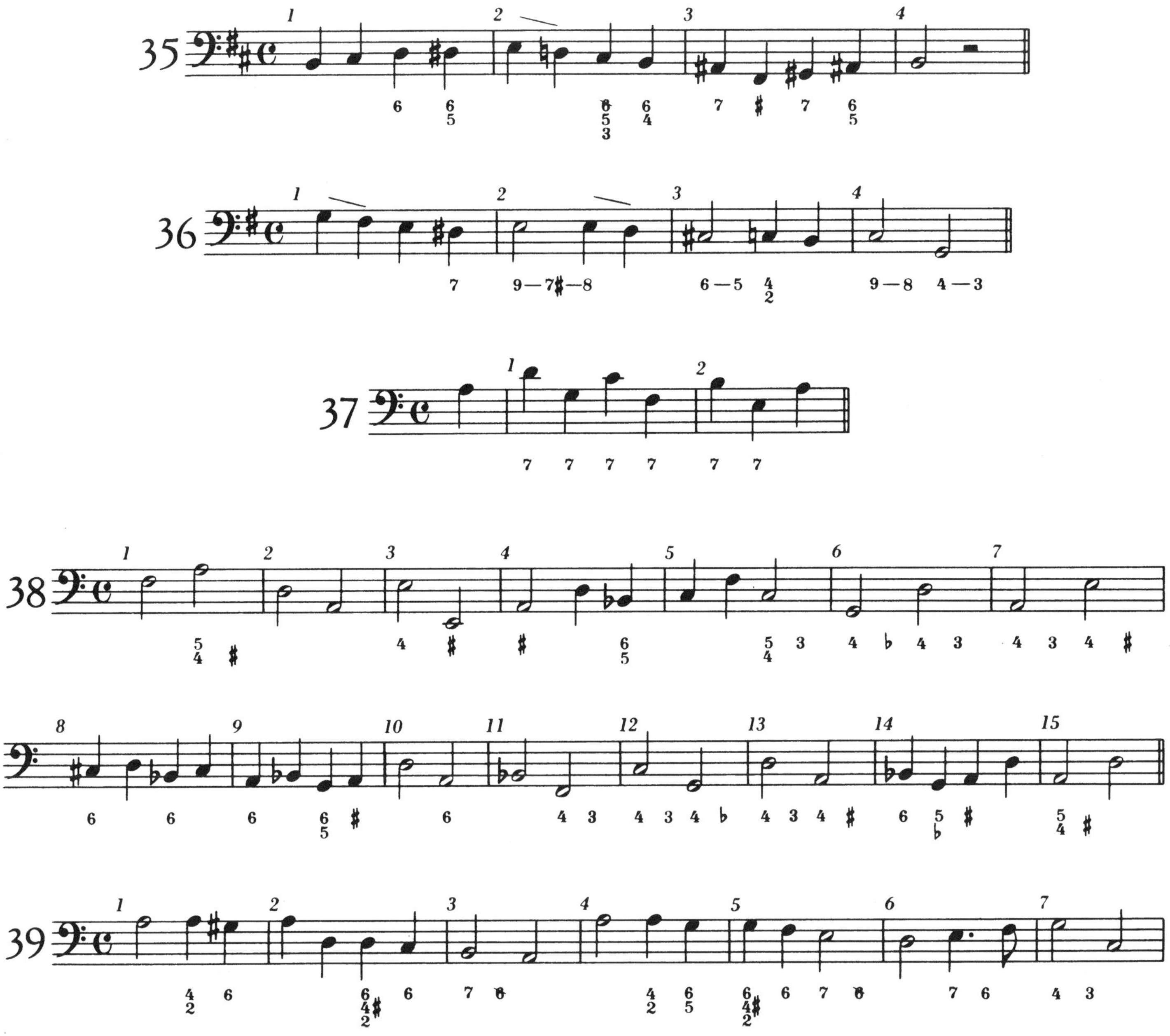
35
36
37
38
39

212

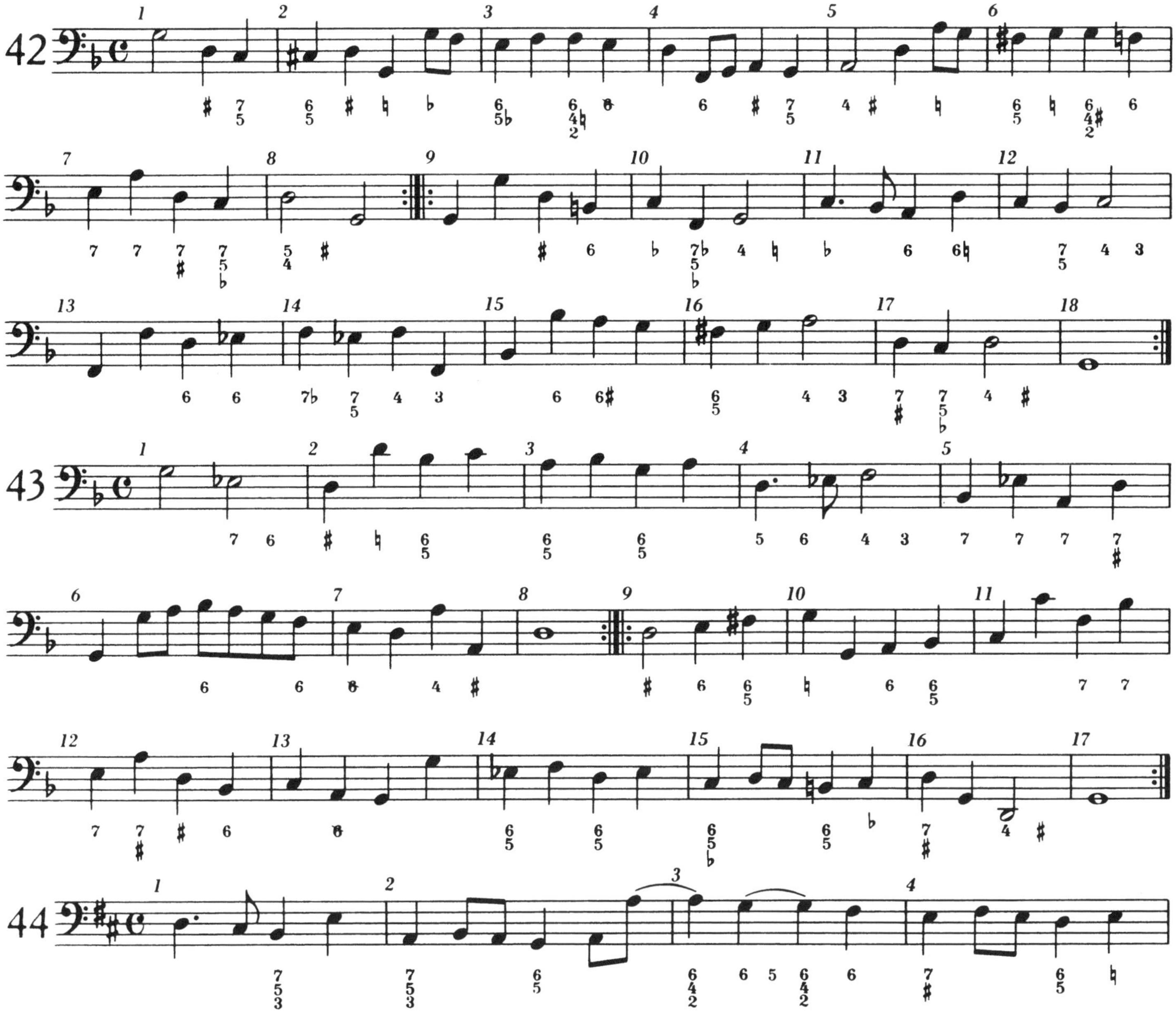
42
43
44

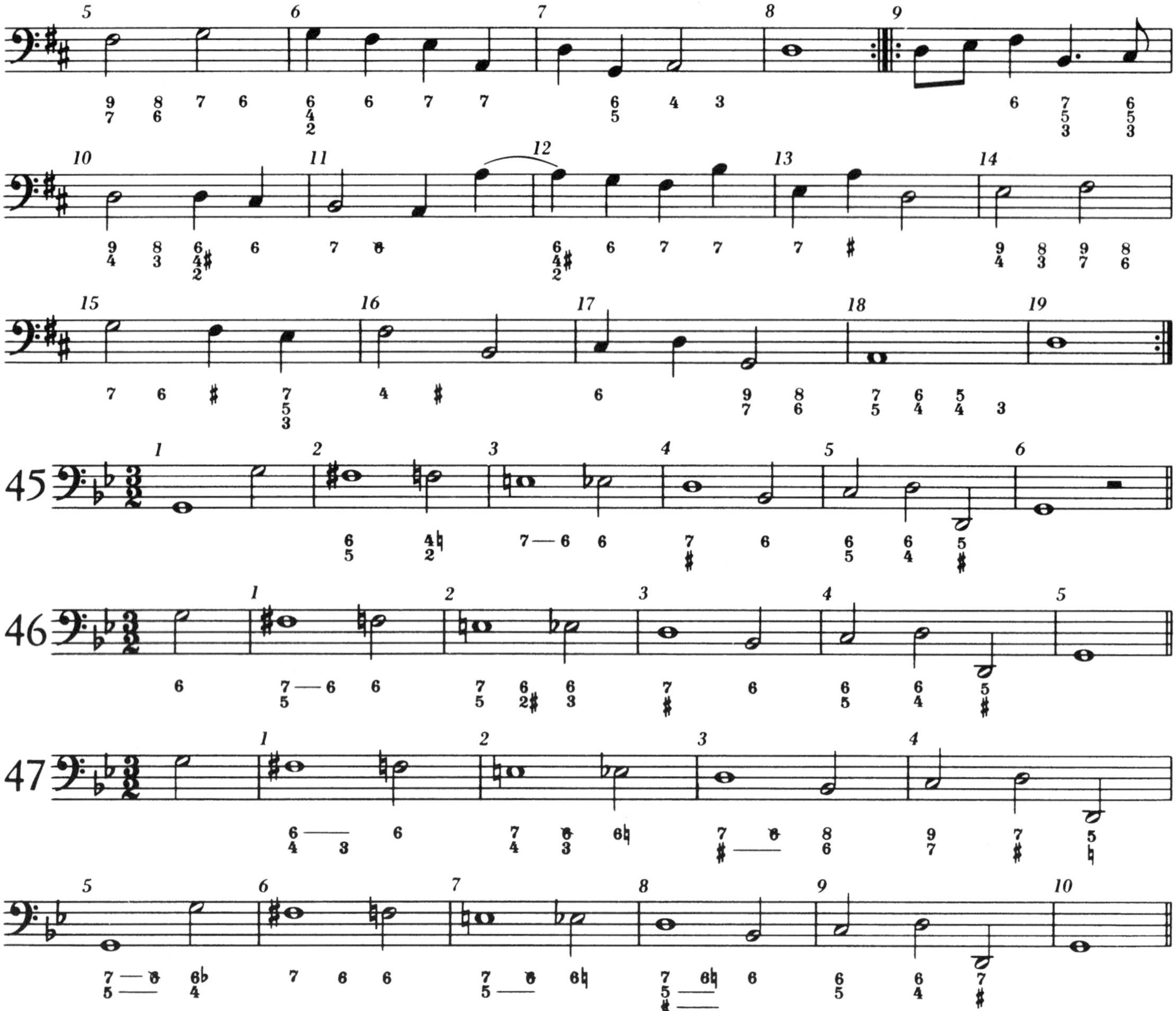
45
46
47

48

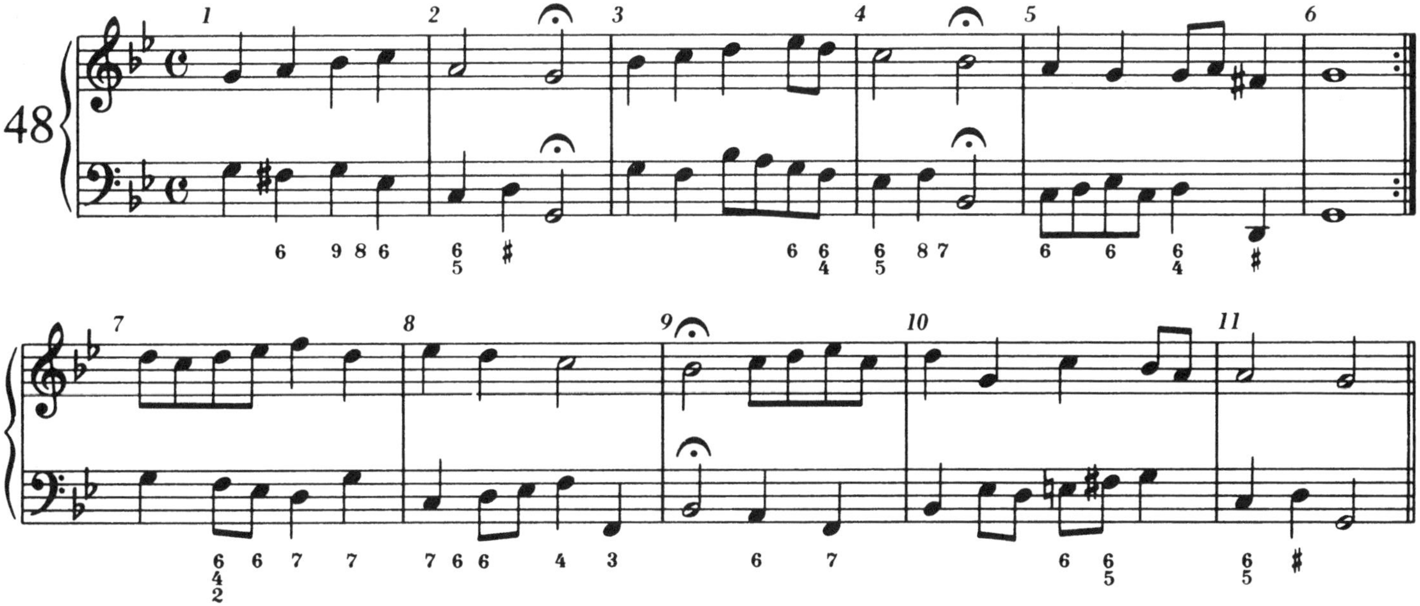

49

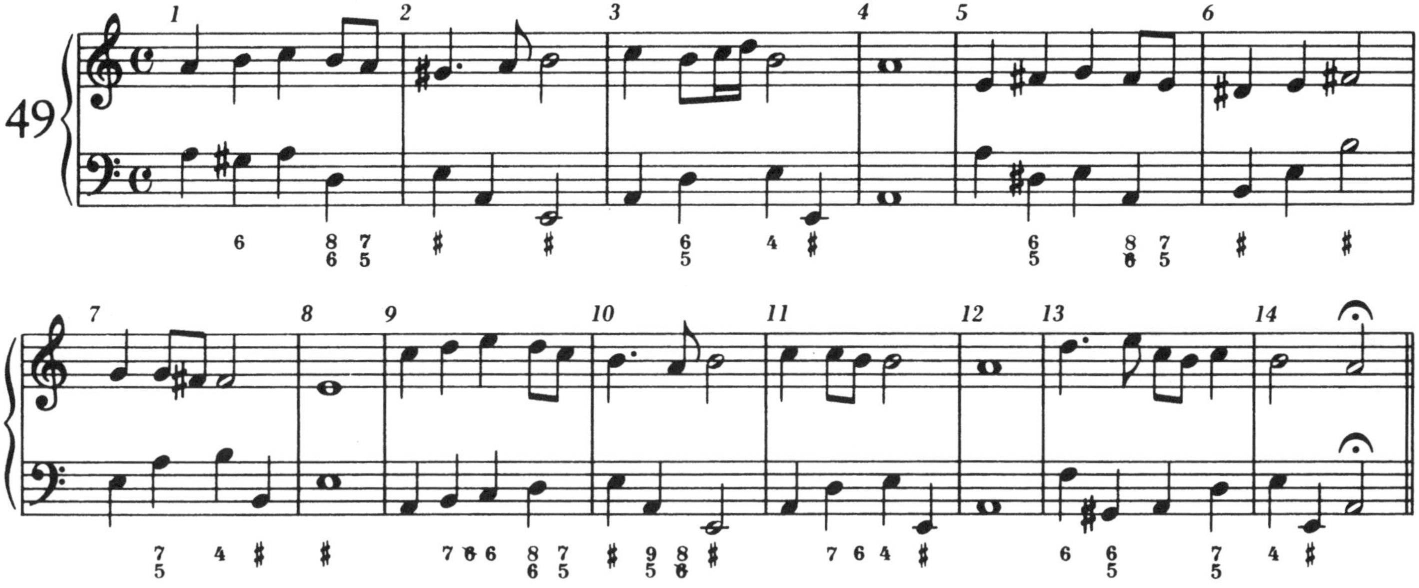

50

51

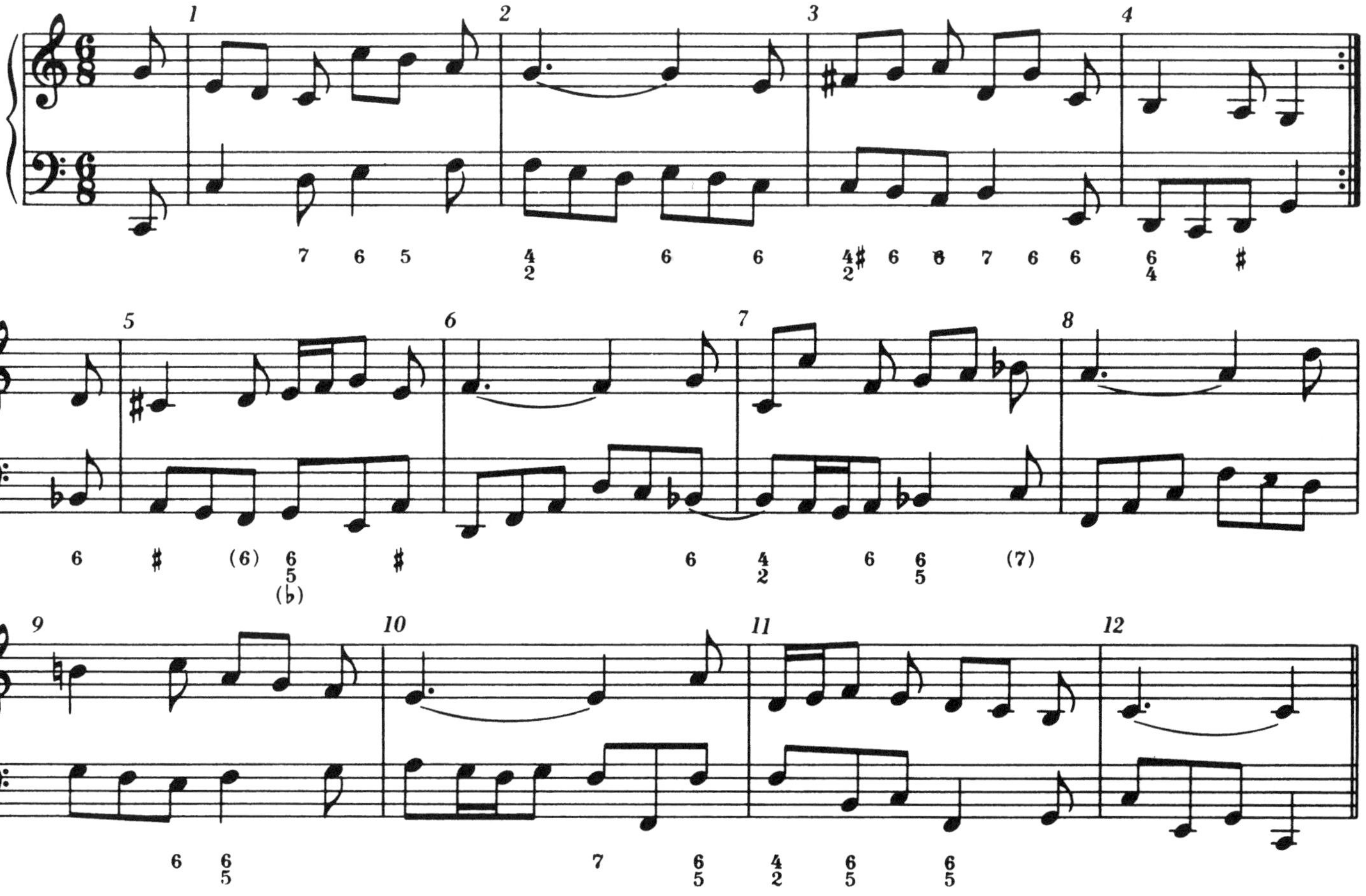

52

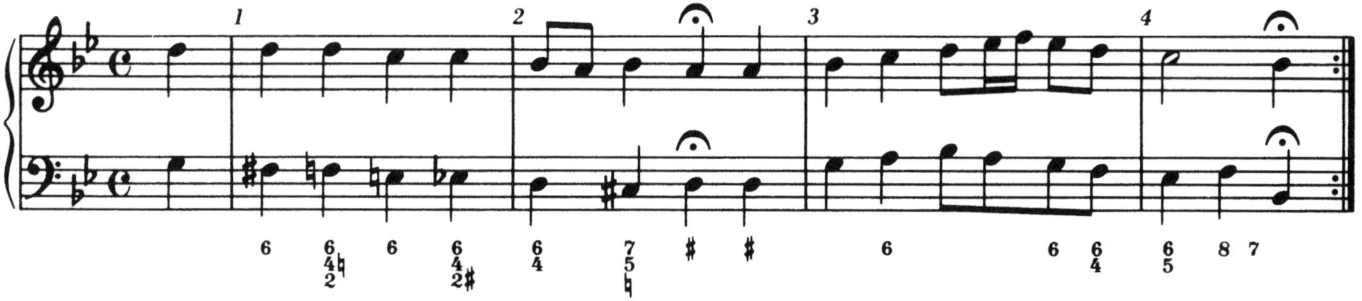

218

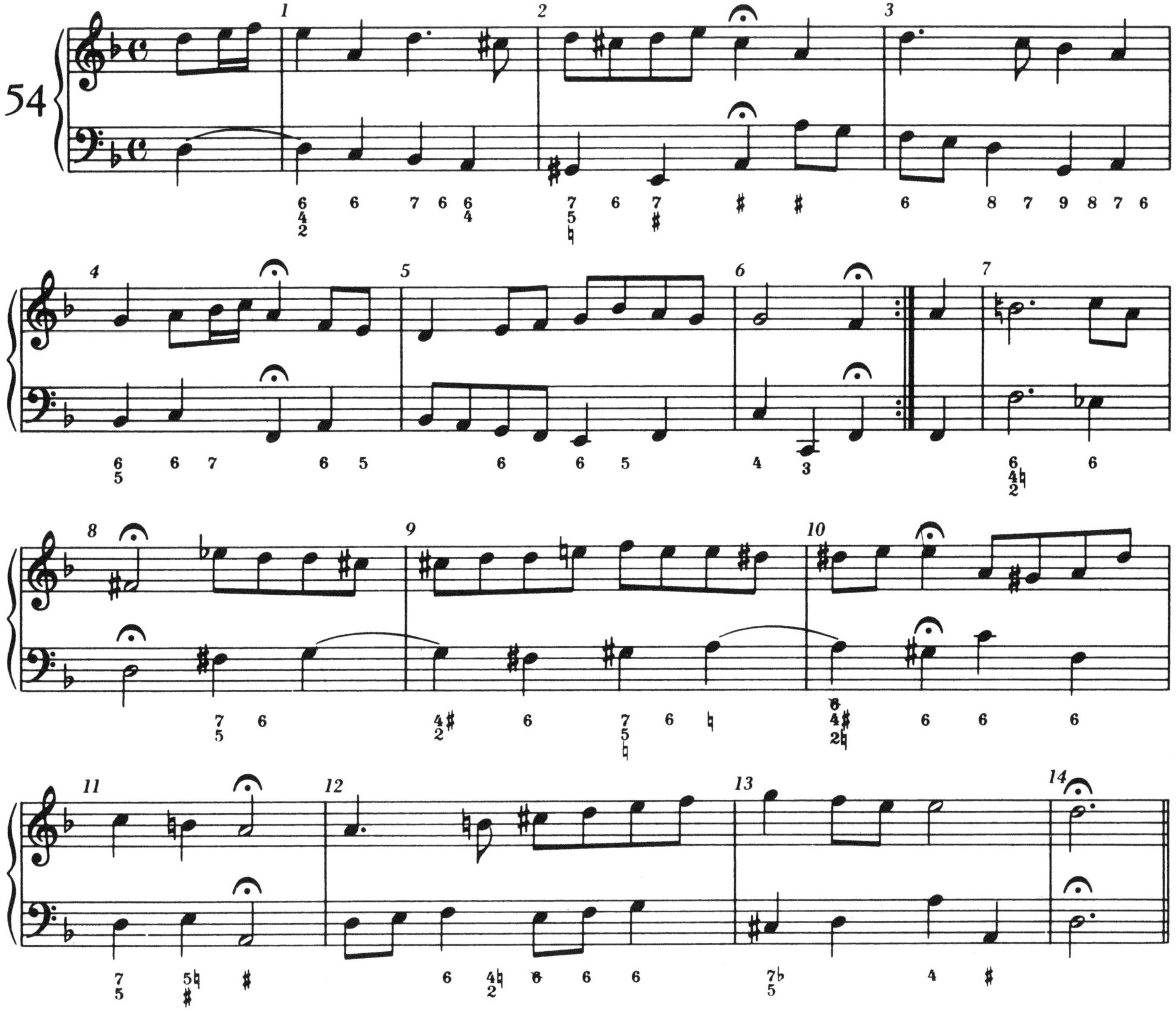